✤

Cooking in a Castle

✤

Cooking
in a
Castle

La Cuisine dans un Château

❖ ❖ ❖ ❖ ❖ ❖ ❖ ❖ ❖ ❖ ❖ ❖ ❖ ❖ ❖

THE ROYAL RECIPES OF FRANCE

WILLIAM I. KAUFMAN
PHOTOGRAPHS BY WILLIAM I. KAUFMAN

BONANZA BOOKS   •   NEW YORK

Other Cookbooks by
WILLIAM I. KAUFMAN

THE CATHOLIC COOKBOOK

THE ART OF INDIA'S COOKERY

THE ART OF CREOLE COOKERY

THE COFFEE COOKBOOK

THE NUT COOKBOOK

THE I LOVE PEANUT BUTTER COOKBOOK

THE SUGAR FREE COOKBOOK

THE SUGAR FREE COOKBOOK OF FAMILY FAVORITES

THE WONDERFUL WORLD OF COOKING:

1 NEAR-EAST, FAR-EAST

2 CARIBBEAN—LATIN AMERICA

3 ITALY, FRANCE AND SPAIN

4 NORTHERN EUROPE AND THE BRITISH ISLES

LIBRARY OF CONGRESS CATALOG CARD NUMBER: 65–23936

This edition published by Bonanza Books,
a division of Crown Publishers, Inc.,
by arrangement with the author

a   b   c   d   e   f   g   h

DESIGNED BY BEN FEDER, INC.

PRINTED IN THE UNITED STATES OF AMERICA

✤

Cooking in a Castle

La Cuisine dans un Château

✤

IS DEDICATED TO

MY WIFE

✤

Contents

INTRODUCTION

COOKING IN A CASTLE is dedicated to sharing some of the secrets of the castle kitchens of Old France with the modern homemaker.

In past centuries the prestige of a castle was, more often than not, based upon the quality of the culinary specialties developed by the chef rather than upon the family name of the lord who owned the most land. The creation of these masterpieces was engendered by the French love of fine food and by the demand for delicacies that were new and exciting to the palate. Because a Seigneur's social standing depended so heavily upon the cuisine of his château, competition was keen for building a reputation for the *bonne table*.

My goal as a cookbook writer has always been to bring to the food connoisseur a new and different taste experience with each succeeding volume, but I did not realize when I initiated COOKING IN A CASTLE how truly different this book would be. As different as red wine from white, as *pâté* from terrine—so the castle-hotels, relais, and historical restaurants represented in this book are different from one another, and so different also are their particular recipes.

The cooking done in each of these kitchens is unique. This follows the pattern of history; the more illustrious and deluxe the château, the wider the range of foods; the more sumptuous the environment, the greater the stress on *haute cuisine*. The smaller châteaux feature the more regional cuisine.

The recipes in this book present a broad variety of foods, and they have been arranged in a manner which makes them easy to prepare. The reader will not be expected to go into the fields to collect herbs and spices, as did the chef of ancient times. The modern cook need only decide what size container to select from a well-stocked market shelf.

In order to collect the recipes, the history, and photographs in this volume, I spent several unforgettable months driving thousands of miles throughout France with my wife as the interpreter of countless conversations. In addition to introducing the precious culinary secrets I found, I hope to share with the reader the pleasure of discovering that one may spend the night or a week in these glorious domains, once frequented only by the royal and privileged.

In doing the research necessary to this book, it was fascinating to sleep one night in what seven hundred years ago was the counting room of the powerful lords of Les Baux, and then, some nights later, to find myself on the site of the storied romance between Marie, the Princess of Monaco, and her handsome but unfaithful lover, the Prince de Condé.

We dined in rare atmospheres. We supped in medieval rooms dug into the top of a mountain. We enjoyed the refreshing coolness of vouted guard rooms. We ate in the luxurious palace of the archbishops of Cahors, and we dined on the terrace once paced by Cardinal Richelieu. Adding to the allure of our meals were beautiful castle gardens from which were plucked the flowers which brightened our rooms and enhanced the food presentations. Our breakfast trays were gay with blossoms.

The scenery contributed greatly to our dining pleasure. High over the southern coast of France, for example, we ate dinner by candlelight, watching below us the sparkling lights of Nice, Cannes, and Monte Carlo. And dinner atop the cliffs of the Loire was glorified by the sweeping panorama of the river meandering to the horizon.

All of this—the castles, the dining rooms, the profusion of flowers, the pervading sense of history, and above all, the delectable foods— played an important role in giving me the enthusiasm and joy that I want to pass on to you, the Reader. My hope is that you will be inspired not only to use the recipes from COOKING IN A CASTLE, but also to visit and bask in the luxurious tranquillity of these magnificent château-hotels and relais. Then, when you return home, you may wish to perpetuate this pleasure by cooking the memorable dishes you have enjoyed.

—William I. Kaufman

Hors d' Oeuvre
and
Canapés

Château de Betz

✦ ✦ ✦

LOBSTER PATTIES

Bouchées de Homard Princesse

MEAT FROM ONE FRESH-COOKED
LOBSTER
1 COOKED POTATO, RICED

2 TEASPOONS ANCHOVY BUTTER
1 TEASPOON GRATED ONION
1 EGG, BEATEN

SALT AND PEPPER

Put lobster meat through food chopper or mince. Combine with potato, anchovy butter, onion, egg, and salt and pepper to taste. Form into balls; chill. When ready to serve, deep-fry at 290°F. 2 minutes.

YIELD: APPETIZER SERVINGS FOR 16

Château de la Tortinière

✦ ✦ ✦

LOBSTER COCKTAIL

Mayonnaise de Homard

2 POUNDS COLD, COOKED LOBSTER
MEAT, COARSELY CUT
1 CUP COOKED CRAB MEAT, BONED
AND FLAKED
1½ CUPS DICED CUCUMBER
1¼ CUPS MAYONNAISE, DIVIDED
LETTUCE
2 TABLESPOONS TOMATO PASTE

1 TABLESPOON TARRAGON
VINEGAR
¼ CUP CHILI SAUCE
1 TEASPOON ONION JUICE
1 TABLESPOON CHOPPED PARSLEY
1 TABLESPOON CHOPPED CHIVES
¼ CUP WHIPPED CREAM
DASH CAYENNE

1 TEASPOON GIN

Combine lobster meat, crab meat, cucumber, and ¼ cup of the mayonnaise. Chill. When ready to serve, line cocktail glasses with lettuce leaves; spoon in lobster mixture. Combine remaining 1 cup mayonnaise with remaining ingredients for sauce. Spoon over top.

YIELD: APPROXIMATELY 8 TO 12 SERVINGS

Château d' Ayres

✦ ✦ ✦

SPICED COCKTAIL BALLS

Boulettes à la Diable

1 CAN (6 OUNCES) BONED CHICKEN, MINCED

2 TABLESPOONS FINELY CHOPPED CELERY

2 TABLESPOONS FINELY CHOPPED CHIVES

PREPARED MUSTARD

1 TABLESPOON FINELY CHOPPED PARSLEY

2 TABLESPOONS FINELY DICED FRESH BREAD CRUMBS

1 TABLESPOON GRATED ONION

1 TABLESPOON CURRY POWDER

1 EGG, BEATEN WITH CREAM

Combine all ingredients using enough mustard to bind together. Form into small balls. Roll in fine dry bread crumbs, then dip in beaten egg diluted with a little cream, then roll in crumbs again. Chill. When ready to serve, deep-fry at 290°F. 2 minutes.

YIELD: APPETIZER SERVINGS FOR 6

La Petite Auberge de Noves

✦ ✦ ✦

COLD SOUFFLÉ PROVENÇAL

Soufflé Glacé Provençal

2 TABLESPOONS CHOPPED PARSLEY

2 TABLESPOONS CHOPPED CHERVIL

1 TEASPOON CHOPPED TARRAGON

2 CUPS CHICKEN STOCK

6 EGGS, SEPARATED

2 CUPS TOMATO PURÉE

1 TEASPOON MINCED GARLIC

SALT AND PEPPER

⅛ TEASPOON ALLSPICE

2 CUPS WHIPPED CREAM

2 CUPS PEELED AND DICED TOMATOES

1 POUND COOKED HAM, FINELY DICED

12 BAKED PASTRY SHELLS

Put parsley, chervil, tarragon, and stock in saucepan. Cover. Bring to a boil. Simmer a few minutes. Put egg yolks in a bowl and beat slightly. Add hot liquid, stirring constantly. Add the tomato purée, garlic, salt, pepper, and allspice. Beat egg whites stiff but not dry. Fold into mixture; fold in whipped cream. Stir in diced tomatoes and ham. Put in refrigerator until cool. Pour into pastry shells. Serve cold.

YIELD: 12 SERVINGS

Château de Challes

✢ ✢ ✢

PIQUANT PATTIES

Bouchées Piquantes

1 PACKAGE (8 OUNCES) CREAM
  CHEESE
2 TEASPOONS DRAINED PREPARED
  HORSERADISH
2 TEASPOONS FINELY CHOPPED
  DILL PICKLE

2 TEASPOONS DRAINED CHOPPED
  CAPERS
1 TEASPOON MINCED ALMONDS
1 TABLESPOON MINCED PARSLEY
1 TABLESPOON CHOPPED CHIVES
  GROUND NUTS

FINELY CHOPPED PARSLEY

Combine cream cheese with horseradish, pickle, capers, almonds, parsley, and chives. Form into ½-inch balls. Roll in ground nuts mixed with finely chopped parsley. Chill.

YIELD: APPETIZER SERVINGS FOR 6

Château de la Chèvre d'Or

✢ ✢ ✢

ANCHOVY CRUSTS

Croûtes d'Anchois

1½ DOZEN ANCHOVY FILLETS,
  DIVIDED
  2 HARD-COOKED EGGS

½ TEASPOON CURRY POWDER
  SOFTENED BUTTER
3 BREAD SLICES

Mash 9 of the anchovy fillets to a fine paste with egg yolks and curry powder and enough butter for spreading consistency. Trim crust from bread slices; toast under broiler on one side and cut each slice into 3 strips. Spread anchovy mixture on untoasted sides; top each with remaining anchovies; sprinkle each with a few drops lemon juice. Finely chop egg whites; use to border strips. Sprinkle with paprika. Bake in a 425°F. oven, 2 to 3 minutes.

YIELD: 2 SERVINGS

Hostellerie du Prieuré

✦ ✦ ✦

COUNTRY STYLE PÂTÉ

Terrine Campagnarde

2 POUNDS PORK TENDERLOIN,
  CUT INTO 2-INCH SQUARES
2 POUNDS BONELESS LEAN VEAL,
  CUT INTO 2-INCH SQUARES
3 SHALLOTS, CHOPPED
1 LARGE ONION, CHOPPED
1 GARLIC CLOVE, MASHED
1 BOUQUET GARNI*

1 LARGE CARROT, THINLY SLICED
1 TEASPOON SALT
8 PEPPERCORNS
½ CUP OLIVE OIL
2 CUPS SAUTERNE WINE
  SAUSAGE AND PORK CRACKLING
  SLICED MUSHROOMS AND
  TRUFFLES

Put all except last 4 ingredients into a large bowl. Cover; refrigerate 24 hours, stirring occasionally. Line an earthenware casserole with thin sheets of larding pork; pack in the drained meat pieces. Fill the spaces with equal parts of pieces of sausage and pork crackling, sliced mushrooms and truffles. Pour in the strained marinade. Top with sheets of larding pork. Cover. Bake in a 375°F. oven, 4 hours. Cool 48 hours before eating. This *pâté* will keep well in the refrigerator several weeks.

YIELD: 4 POUNDS

*A *bouquet garni* is a combination of parsley, thyme, and bay leaf, used for flavoring and usually tied in a piece of cheesecloth so that it can be removed easily.

Château de la Vallée Bleue

✦ ✦ ✦

CANTALOUPE ESCOFFIER

Melons Escoffier

3 CANTALOUPE
1 SMALL PINEAPPLE

1 PINT STRAWBERRIES
½ CUP KIRSCH, BRANDY, OR RUM

Cut off top from stem end of cantaloupe; reserve. Spoon out seeds and membrane. Pare and dice pineapple; wash, hull, and halve strawberries. Combine both and spoon into cantaloupe cavities. Pour in kirsch; cover with reserved tops. Chill. When ready to serve cut each melon in half; remove tops. Serve with whipped cream.

YIELD: 6 SERVINGS

Château de la Vallée Bleue

✦ ✦ ✦

HORSERADISH FRITTERS

Beignets au Raifort

¼ CUP FINELY SCRAPED FRESH
   HORSERADISH
3 TABLESPOONS HEAVY CREAM
½ POUND BUTTER

3 EGG YOLKS, SLIGHTLY BEATEN
¼ TEASPOON SALT
   DASH CAYENNE
¼ TEASPOON LEMON JUICE

Soak horseradish in heavy cream. Divide butter into 3 equal parts. Put one part in top of double boiler with egg yolks, salt, cayenne, and lemon juice. Cook over simmering water until blended, stirring constantly. Add second portion of butter, bit by bit, stirring constantly. Add last portion all at once, and continue cooking, stirring constantly until mixture just begins to thicken. Remove from water immediately. Add horse-radish and cream and beat until mixture is thick. Spread out thinly on a platter and refrigerate. When ready to serve cut into squares. Dip into sieved bread crumbs, then in Sherry Batter, then into sieved bread crumbs. Deep-fry at 385°F. until golden brown. Drain on absorbent paper.

YIELD: 4 SERVINGS

SHERRY BATTER

Pâte au Xérès

1⅓ CUPS SIFTED ALL-PURPOSE
   FLOUR
2 TEASPOONS BAKING POWDER
¼ TEASPOON SALT
⅓ CUP MILK

   DASH NUTMEG
1 EGG
1 EGG YOLK
1 TABLESPOON SHERRY WINE

Sift flour, baking powder, salt, and nutmeg into a mixing bowl. Beat together whole egg, egg yolk, and sherry. Add alternately with milk to batter, beating after each addition, until smooth.

Soups

Château d'Artigny

❖ ❖ ❖

OYSTER BISQUE

Bisque aux Huîtres

1 QUART OYSTERS
2 CUPS CHICKEN STOCK OR
  BOUILLON
1½ CUPS STALE BREAD CRUMBS
1 SMALL ONION, SLICED

2 CELERY STALKS, WITH LEAVES,
  CHOPPED
1 BOUQUET GARNI
1 QUART MILK, SCALDED
1 TABLESPOON BUTTER

3 TABLESPOONS SHERRY WINE

Cut thin edges from whole oysters; reserve. Chop oysters; place in a deep kettle with oyster liquor. Add chicken stock, bread crumbs, onion, celery, and *bouquet garni*. Bring to a boil; reduce heat and simmer 30 minutes. Strain entire stock into a kettle; add reserved trimmings from oysters. Season to taste with salt, white pepper, and nutmeg. Heat, but do not boil. Add scalded milk, butter, and sherry; heat.

YIELD: 8 to 10 SERVINGS

Château de Coudrée

❖ ❖ ❖

OYSTER SOUP ORLEANAISE

Soupe aux Huîtres Orléanaise

1 QUART OYSTERS
1 QUART MILK, SCALDED
1 SMALL ONION, THINLY SLICED
⅓ CUP FINELY CHOPPED CELERY
4 SPRIGS PARSLEY

1 BAY LEAF
DASH MACE
⅓ CUP BUTTER
⅓ CUP FLOUR
½ CUP HEAVY CREAM

2 EGG YOLKS, SLIGHTLY BEATEN

Drain oysters; reserve liquor. Chop oysters and place them in saucepan with their liquor. Bring to a boil; reduce heat and simmer 10 minutes. While mixture is simmering, scald milk with onion, celery, parsley, bay leaf, and a dash of mace. Strain. Melt butter in a deep saucepan; blend in flour. Gradually add oysters with liquor and strained milk. Cook, stirring constantly, until mixture thickens and comes to a boil. Remove from heat; stir in heavy cream combined with egg yolks. Season to taste with salt and white pepper. Strain into soup tureen. Serve with Melba toast.

YIELD: 6 SERVINGS

Château de Pray

✦ ✦ ✦

CREAM OF MUSHROOM AND SHERRY SOUP

Potage Crème de Champignons au Xérès

3 TABLESPOONS BUTTER
3 TABLESPOONS FLOUR
1 TEASPOON SALT
¼ TEASPOON DRY MUSTARD
DASH CAYENNE
1 QUART CHICKEN STOCK

¾ POUND MUSHROOMS, CLEANED
AND CHOPPED
⅓ CUP SHERRY WINE
½ CUP HEAVY CREAM, SCALDED
WHIPPED CREAM
TOASTED SLIVERED ALMONDS

Melt butter in a deep saucepan. Blend in flour, salt, mustard, and cayenne. Gradually add chicken stock and cook, stirring constantly, until mixture thickens and comes to a boil. Add mushrooms. Reduce heat and simmer 40 minutes. Strain; stir in wine and cream. Top each serving with a spoonful of whipped cream and sprinkle with toasted slivered almonds.

YIELD: 4 TO 6 SERVINGS

Château Choiseul

✦ ✦ ✦

CREAM OF SPINACH SOUP

Potage Crème d' Épinards

1 POUND SPINACH
3 TABLESPOONS BUTTER
2 TABLESPOONS FINELY CHOPPED
ONION

3 TABLESPOONS FLOUR
1½ CUPS MILK
SALT, PEPPER, GROUND NUTMEG
2 EGG YOLKS, SLIGHTLY BEATEN
¾ CUP HEAVY CREAM

Wash spinach thoroughly; place in a saucepan without adding water. Cover; cook over low heat 10 minutes, stirring once. Remove from heat; drain and reserve liquid. Force spinach through a sieve. Melt butter in a deep saucepan; add onion and cook until tender. Blend in flour. Gradually add milk and cook, stirring constantly, until mixture thickens and comes to a boil. Add strained spinach and liquid. Season to taste with salt, pepper, and nutmeg. Simmer until mixture is heated through. Beat egg yolks with cream. Add to spinach mixture, stirring rapidly, until mixture is slightly thickened.

YIELD: 4 TO 6 SERVINGS

Hostellerie de la Poste

❖ ❖ ❖

CREAM OF ASPARAGUS SOUP

Potage Crème d' Asperges

1 BUNCH FRESH ASPARAGUS
1 MEDIUM ONION, SLICED
1 BOUQUET GARNI
3 TABLESPOONS BUTTER
3 TABLESPOONS FLOUR

½ TEASPOON SALT
⅛ TEASPOON PEPPER
1½ CUPS MILK
2 EGG YOLKS, SLIGHTLY BEATEN
  GROUND NUTMEG

Wash asparagus; cut off woody ends; discard. Cut asparagus into 1-inch pieces. Remove 1 cup and cook until tender; reserve. Place remaining asparagus into a deep saucepan. Add onion, *boquet garni,* and enough water to barely cover. Bring to a boil. Reduce heat and simmer 25 minutes, or until asparagus is tender. Drain. Force asparagus through a sieve; reserve. Melt butter in a deep saucepan. Blend in flour, salt and pepper. Add milk and cook, stirring constantly, until mixture thickens and comes to a boil. Remove from heat; add egg yolks, stirring rapidly. Stir in strained asparagus mixture, asparagus pieces, and water in which they were cooked. Heat to serving temperature. To serve, sprinkle with nutmeg.

YIELD: 4 TO 6 SERVINGS

Château de Cheronnac

❖ ❖ ❖

CREAM OF CUCUMBER SOUP

Potage Crème de Concombres

4 MEDIUM CUCUMBERS
1 TABLESPOON BUTTER
3 CUPS CHICKEN STOCK

1 TABLESPOON ONION JUICE
1 CUP HEAVY CREAM
3 EGG YOLKS, SLIGHTLY BEATEN

Peel cucumbers; remove seeds and dice cucumber. Put into a deep saucepan with butter, chicken stock, and onion juice. Bring to a boil. Cover; reduce heat and simmer until cucumber is tender and transparent. Force through a sieve into a saucepan. Season to taste with salt and pepper. Stir in cream; heat. When ready to serve, add egg yolks, stirring rapidly. Heat, but do not boil. Garnish each serving with finely minced chervil or parsley. Soup may also be served chilled.

YIELD: 4 TO 6 SERVINGS

Le Prieuré

✦ ✦ ✦

CHESTNUT SOUP OF THE AUVERGNE

Potage de Châtaignes à l'Auvergnate

1¾ POUNDS CHESTNUTS	DASH BAKING SODA
1 BOUQUET GARNI	⅓ CUP SHERRY WINE
1 QUART CHICKEN STOCK	2 EGG WHITES
1 CUP HEAVY CREAM	DASH SALT
¼ TEASPOON DRY MUSTARD	3 TABLESPOONS GROUND NUTS

Make slits in chestnuts; spread in shallow pan. Bake in a 450°F. oven, 15 minutes; cool. Shell and skin chestnuts. Place in a deep saucepan with *bouquet garni*. Add enough water to cover. Bring to a boil. Cover; reduce heat and simmer 20 to 25 minutes, or until nuts are tender. Drain; force chestnuts through a sieve into a deep saucepan. Add chicken stock. Bring to a boil; add heavy cream, mustard, and soda. Bring to a boil again; remove from heat. Stir in sherry; keep warm. Beat egg whites until stiff, but not dry. Gradually add salt and beat until very stiff. Fold in nuts. Drop by spoonfuls on brown paper on baking sheet; place under broiler until lightly browned. Spoon soup into bouillon cups; top each with a meringue.

YIELD: 8 SERVINGS

Château de la Tortinière

✦ ✦ ✦

ALMOND SOUP

Potage au Lait d'Amandes

1½ POUNDS SWEET ALMONDS, BLANCHED AND SKINNED	1 TEASPOON SALT
1 DOZEN BITTER ALMONDS, BLANCHED AND SKINNED	1 THIN LEMON PEEL
	½ TEASPOON GROUND CORIANDER
6 CUPS WATER	2 EGG YOLKS, SLIGHTLY BEATEN
	MELBA TOAST

Put almonds through a food chopper several times, using finest blade. Put water into a deep saucepan; add salt, lemon peel, and coriander. Gradually add the almond paste, stirring constantly. Boil 5 minutes without stirring. Strain through cheesecloth into top of a double boiler. Keep warm over hot water. When ready to serve, add egg yolks, stirring rapidly. Add additional seasoning if necessary. Spoon over Melba toast.

YIELD: 4 TO 6 SERVINGS

Fish

teau de Betz

✤ ✤ ✤

R   *Homard Thermidor*

KED   2 TABLESPOONS SHERRY WINE,
                        DIVIDED
PS, SLICED   1¼ CUPS LIGHT CREAM, DIVIDED
                    2 EGG YOLKS

lobster. Halve shell; remove meat and reserve
ove meat from claws and coarsely chop all lobster
a saucepan. Add lobster meat and mushrooms and
saute ⌐   ring occasionally. Stir in paprika; salt and pepper to
taste. Add 1 tⁱⁿ spoon of the sherry and ½ cup of the cream, stirring
constantly. Simmer 5 minutes. Beat together remaining sherry, cream
and egg yolks. Add to lobster mixture, beating constantly, but do not boil.
Spoon into lobster shells. Place under broiler until glazed.

YIELD: 2 SERVINGS

Château d'Artigny

✤ ✤ ✤

LOBSTER BERCY   *Homard Bercy*

3 TABLESPOONS BUTTER	1 TABLESPOON MINCED PARSLEY
2 TABLESPOONS MINCED SHALLOT	3 LOBSTERS, COOKED
¾ CUP WHITE WINE	1 SMALL GARLIC CLOVE, MASHED
¾ CUP FISH STOCK	3 SPRIGS PARSLEY
2 CUPS FISH VELOUTÉ*	DASH THYME
½ CUP BUTTER, DIVIDED	8 TABLESPOONS GRATED SWISS CHEESE, DIVIDED

Melt 3 tablespoons butter in a saucepan; add shallot and cook until tender.
Add wine and fish stock and cook until mixture is reduced to one-third its
original volume. Add Fish Velouté; bring to a boil; boil 2 minutes. Stir
in ¼ cup of the butter and parsley; reserve. Split lobsters in two; remove
meat and reserve the juice (there should be about ¼ cup). Chop the lobster meat and sauté in remaining ¼ cup butter with garlic, parsley, and
thyme. Fill the empty shells with half the lobster meat and sprinkle each
with 1 teaspoon of the grated cheese. Top with half the sauce, remaining
lobster, and then remaining sauce. Sprinkle each with 1 tablespoon of the
grated cheese. Place under broiler until lightly browned.

YIELD: 6 SERVINGS

*See page 28

FISH VELOUTÉ

Velouté de Poissons

3 TABLESPOONS BUTTER   3 TABLESPOONS FLOUR

2 CUPS FISH STOCK

Melt butter in a saucepan; blend in flour. Gradually add fish stock and cook, stirring constantly, until mixture comes to a boil. Reduce heat and simmer 15 to 20 minutes. Strain and season to taste with salt and white pepper.

Château de la Chèvre d'Or

✦ ✦ ✦

LOBSTER CASSEROLE

Cassolette de Homard

3 1½-POUND LOBSTERS, COOKED   2 TABLESPOONS BUTTER
2½ CUPS WATER   2 TABLESPOONS FLOUR
½ CARROT, SLICED   ½ CUP HEAVY CREAM
3 ONION SLICES   2 EGG YOLKS, SLIGHTLY BEATEN
3 SPRIGS PARSLEY   ¾ CUP HOT, COOKED RICE
1 SMALL STALK CELERY, CHOPPED   6 BROILED TOMATO SLICES
ANCHOVY BUTTER

Remove meat from lobsters; cut into small pieces. Put shells and small claws from lobsters into a deep saucepan. Add water, carrot, and onion slices, parsley and celery. Bring to a boil; boil until liquid is reduced to 1½ cups. Remove from heat; strain through cheesecloth. Melt butter in a saucepan; blend in flour. Gradually add stock and cook, stirring constantly, until mixture thickens and comes to a boil. Remove from heat. Blend together cream and egg yolks; add to stock, stirring rapidly. Season to taste with salt, white pepper, paprika, and a dash of cayenne. Stir in lobster; mix well. Return to heat; heat to serving temperature. Spoon 2 tablespoons of the rice into 6 individual casseroles; divide lobster mixture among casseroles. Top each with a hot broiled tomato slice. Brush tomato with melted anchovy butter, if desired.

YIELD: 6 SERVINGS

Château de Divonne

✦ ✦ ✦

BRITTANY LOBSTER CASSEROLES

Homard en Timbales à la Bretonne

½ CUP BUTTER
6 SMALL LOBSTERS
2 CUPS DRY CIDER
¼ CUP CALVADOS OR APPLEJACK
2 EGG YOLKS, SLIGHTLY BEATEN

½ CUP HEAVY CREAM, SCALDED
1 TEASPOON EACH FINELY
  CHOPPED CHIVES AND ONION
1 POUND MUSHROOMS, SLICED
  AND COOKED

GRATED SWISS CHEESE

Melt butter in a large, deep skillet; add live lobsters and cook, shaking pan frequently and turning lobsters until they begin to turn red. Add cider and calvados. Cover and cook 20 minutes; turning lobsters occasionally. Drain lobsters; reserve liquid. Crack lobsters; remove meat and cut in small pieces; reserve. Boil reserved liquid until reduced to ½ cup. Add egg yolks to scalded cream, stirring rapidly. Quickly stir into reduced stock over low heat; add chives and onion. Season to taste with salt and pepper. Alternate lobster meat and cooked mushrooms in layers in individual casseroles until almost full, pouring small amount sauce over each layer. Sprinkle each with 1 tablespoon grated cheese. Place under broiler until lightly browned.

YIELD: 6 TO 8 SERVINGS

Château d'Ayres

✦ ✦ ✦

LOBSTER SALAD HOMESTYLE

Salade de Homard Chez Soi

3 CUPS COOKED, COARSELY CUT
   LOBSTER MEAT
¾ CUP SLICED CELERY
½ CUP DICED GREEN PEPPER
½ CUP DICED APPLE
1 BAY LEAF
¾ CUP FRENCH DRESSING
⅓ CUP MAYONNAISE
1 TABLESPOON BOTTLED THICK
   MEAT SAUCE

2 TABLESPOONS CATCHUP
1 TEASPOON WORCESTERSHIRE
   SAUCE
1 TABLESPOON PREPARED MUSTARD
1 TEASPOON CHOPPED PARSLEY
1 TEASPOON MINCED ONION
1 TEASPOON FINELY CHOPPED
   CHERVIL OR CHIVES
   CAPERS
   HARD-COOKED EGG SLICES

Combine lobster, celery, green pepper, apple, and bay leaf. Add French dressing and marinate in refrigerator several hours, turning occasionally. Drain marinade; reserve ⅓ cup. To the reserved marinade, add remaining ingredients. Season to taste with salt and pepper and a dash of curry powder. Add 2 to 3 ice cubes and stir until mixture thickens. Remove cubes. Combine with lobster mixture. Pile the lobster mixture into a mound in a bowl lined with salad greens. Spread lobster with a thin layer of mayonnaise. Sprinkle with capers and garnish with hard-cooked halved egg slices, one half of each slice dipped in paprika and the other half dipped in finely chopped parsley.

YIELD: 6 SERVINGS

Château de Betz

✦ ✦ ✦

FRIED SOFT-SHELL CRABS SAUCE VINCENT

Crabes Sauce Vincent

¼ CUP GRATED SWISS CHEESE
1 CUP BECHAMEL SAUCE*
1 DOZEN SOFT-SHELL CRABS

Add grated cheese to hot Bechamel Sauce; stir until cheese is melted. Have crabs cleaned and ready to fry. Sprinkle crabs with salt, pepper, and nutmeg. Dip in flour, then in sauce. Roll in fine dry bread crumbs. Deep-fry at 375°F. until browned. Serve with Sauce Vincent.†

YIELD: 6 SERVINGS

*See page 95 †See page 100

Château de la Chèvre d'Or

✦ ✦ ✦

FROGS LEGS PROVENÇALE BOURGEOISE

Grenouilles à la Provençale

2 DOZEN FROGS LEGS
2 CUPS CHICKEN OR VEAL STOCK
1 BOUQUET GARNI
2 LEMON SLICES
⅓ CUP OLIVE OIL

2 TEASPOONS MINCED SHALLOT
1 TABLESPOON MINCED FRESH
   MUSHROOMS
1 GARLIC CLOVE, MASHED
1 TEASPOON MINCED PARSLEY

1 CAN (6 OUNCES) TOMATO PASTE

Put frogs legs into a deep saucepan; add stock, *bouquet garni,* and lemon slices. Bring to a boil. Cover; reduce heat and simmer 20 minutes. Drain; reserve 1½ cups of the stock. Heat olive oil in a saucepan. Add shallot, mushrooms, garlic, and parsley; cook until tender. Add tomato paste and reserved stock. Simmer 15 minutes. Season to taste with salt and pepper. Combine with frogs legs; heat to serving temperature. Remove *bouquet garni* and lemon slices.

YIELD: 4 SERVINGS

L'Oustau de Baumanière

✦ ✦ ✦

FROGS LEGS IN RED WINE

Grenouilles au Vin Rouge

3 TABLESPOONS BUTTER, DIVIDED
1 SMALL ONION, GRATED
1 TABLESPOON GRATED CARROT
1 GARLIC CLOVE, MASHED

1 BAY LEAF
1 TABLESPOON FLOUR
1 TABLESPOON TOMATO PASTE
2½ DOZEN SMALL FROGS LEGS

1 CUP RED WINE

Melt 2 tablespoons of the butter in a saucepan. Add onion, carrot, garlic, bay leaf, a pinch of marjoram, cloves, thyme, and fennel. Season to taste with salt and pepper. Cook 3 minutes. Cream together remaining butter, flour, and tomato paste. Gradually add to butter mixture, bit by bit, until mixture thickens. Add frogs legs; cook, stirring occasionally, 5 minutes. Add wine and cook, stirring constantly, until mixture comes to a boil. Remove frogs legs; place on toast on serving platter. Spoon sauce over top.

YIELD: 6 SERVINGS

Château de Coudrée

✤ ✤ ✤

FRICASSEE OF FROGS LEGS

Fricassée de Grenouilles en Cassolettes

3 DOZEN FROGS LEGS
WHITE WINE
12 SPRIGS PARSLEY
1 BAY LEAF
1 LARGE GARLIC CLOVE, MASHED
2 WHOLE CLOVES
8 WHOLE PEPPERCORNS
1 SPRIG THYME

1 SMALL ONION, SLICED
5 THIN SLICES CARROT
JUICE OF 1 LEMON
3 SHALLOTS, CHOPPED
2 SPRIGS FENNEL
⅓ CUP BUTTER
1 TABLESPOON FLOUR
3 EGG YOLKS

2 TABLESPOONS TOMATO PASTE

Put frogs legs into a deep bowl. Add enough wine to cover. Stir in parsley, bay leaf, garlic, whole cloves, peppercorns, thyme, onion, carrot, lemon juice, shallots, and fennel. Let marinate 30 minutes, stirring occasionally. Melt butter in a skillet; add drained frogs legs and cook 3 minutes over medium heat, shaking the skillet occasionally. Transfer legs to a shallow baking pan. Blend flour into butter in skillet; gradually strain in marinade. Cook, stirring constantly, until mixture thickens slightly. Pour over frogs legs. Set pan into a larger pan over direct heat. Pour boiling water into larger pan. Let simmer 5 minutes. Beat together egg yolks and tomato paste; stir into the frog mixture. Divide among 6 individual casseroles; place under broiler until lightly browned.

YIELD: 6 SERVINGS

L'Oustau de Baumanière

✤ ✤ ✤

SCALLOPS MORNAY

Coquilles Saint-Jacques Mornay

1 PINT SEA SCALLOPS
1½ CUPS MORNAY SAUCE*
½ CUP SLICED COOKED MUSHROOMS

1 TEASPOON FINELY CHOPPED
SHALLOT
BUTTERED BREAD CRUMBS
GRATED SWISS CHEESE

Coarsely cut scallops; let cook in their own liquor until tender. Drain; add to hot Mornay Sauce with mushrooms and shallot. Spoon into oven-proof shells; sprinkle with crumbs which have been combined with cheese. Place under broiler until lightly browned.

YIELD: 4 SERVINGS

*See page 101

Château de Pray

❖ ❖ ❖

MUSSELS BORDELAISE

Moules Bordelaises

3 QUARTS MUSSELS
¼ TEASPOON THYME
1 BAY LEAF
2 MEDIUM ONIONS, CHOPPED
1 SMALL GARLIC CLOVE
JUICE OF 1 LEMON
3 EGG YOLKS, SLIGHTLY BEATEN

Clean mussels in several changes of water. Place in a deep saucepan with 4 tablespoons boiling water. Add thyme, bay leaf, onion, and garlic. Place over low heat, shaking occasionally, just until the shells open. Remove from heat. In another saucepan, melt 1 teaspoon butter for each dozen mussels. Carefully strain in the mussel liquor. Add salt and pepper to taste and lemon juice; bring to a boil. Remove from heat; add egg yolks, stirring rapidly. Return to heat; heat, but do not boil. Serve over mussels which have been removed from their shells.

YIELD: 6 SERVINGS

Château de la Tortinière

❖ ❖ ❖

OYSTERS IN SHERRY WINE SAUCE

Huîtres aux Croûtons

CRUSTS OF FRENCH BREAD
½ CUP BUTTER
½ TEASPOON ANCHOVY PASTE
2 PINTS OYSTERS, DRAINED
2 TABLESPOONS EACH MINCED
CHIVES, PARSLEY, AND SHALLOTS,
DIVIDED
2 TEASPOONS EACH LIME JUICE
AND GRATED ONION
¾ CUP HEAVY CREAM
2 TABLESPOONS SHERRY WINE
½ CUP BUTTERED BREAD CRUMBS
½ CUP GRATED PARMESAN CHEESE

Trim crust from French bread; cut into ¼-inch cubes to make 1 quart. Melt butter in a large skillet; blend in anchovy paste. Add bread cubes and cook, stirring occasionally, until browned. Season to taste with salt and cayenne. Butter a 3-quart casserole. Put in half the croutons. Top with half of the oysters. Sprinkle with half the chives, parsley, shallots, lime juice, and onion. Repeat layers. Combine cream with sherry; pour over all. Combine buttered bread crumbs and cheese; sprinkle over top. Bake in a 300°F. oven, 35 minutes.

YIELD: 8 TO 10 SERVINGS

Château de Pray

✦ ✦ ✦

OYSTER CHEESE PIE

Quiche aux Huîtres

PASTRY FOR 1 PIE CRUST
1 TABLESPOON MINCED
  SMOKED SALMON
2 PINTS OYSTERS
1 CUP LIGHT CREAM
2 THIN ONION SLICES
1 SMALL BAY LEAF
1 WHOLE CLOVE
4 EGGS
3 TABLESPOON SHERRY WINE
½ CUP GRATED GRUYÈRE OR
  SWISS CHEESE, DIVIDED
1½ TABLESPOONS BUTTER

Roll out pastry; fit into a 9-inch pie plate and flute edges. Pick sides and bottom with a fork. Bake in a 400°F. oven, 10 minutes. Remove from oven; cool. Sprinkle with minced salmon. Drain the oysters; reserve ½ cup liquor. Place half the oysters in bottom of crust. Put cream into a saucepan with onion, bay leaf, and clove; season to taste with salt, white pepper, celery salt, and thyme. Scald; remove from heat. Add oyster liquor. Strain and cool. Beat in eggs, one at a time, beating constantly; stir in sherry. Pour half the mixture into crust; sprinkle with ¼ cup of the cheese and top with remaining oysters. Add remaining sauce and top with cheese. Dot with butter. Bake in a 350°F. oven, 30 minutes, or until top is delicately brown.

YIELD: 6 TO 8 SERVINGS

Château de Betz

✦ ✦ ✦

FRENCH CREAMED OYSTERS

Huîtres à la Crème Française

½ CUP BUTTER
1 TABLESPOON ENGLISH MUSTARD
¼ TEASPOON ANCHOVY PASTE
3 CUPS FINELY CHOPPED CELERY
1 QUART HEAVY CREAM
4 DOZEN OYSTERS WITH LIQUOR
¼ CUP SHERRY WINE
PAPRIKA
GROUND NUTMEG

Melt butter in a deep saucepan with mustard and anchovy paste. Add celery and cook until tender. Season to taste with salt and pepper. Add cream; heat, stirring occasionally until mixture comes to a boil. Add oysters, cook until edges begin to curl. Stir in wine. Serve on hot toast. Sprinkle each serving lightly with paprika and nutmeg.

YIELD: 6 SERVINGS

Château de Cheronnac

✦ ✦ ✦

OYSTERS À LA NANTUA

Huîtres à la Nantua

¾ CUP SHELLED COOKED SHRIMP
¼ CUP BONED COOKED CRABMEAT
¼ CUP BONED COOKED FLOUNDER
 NANTUA SAUCE*
¼ TEASPOON TABASCO

½ TEASPOON WORCESTERSHIRE
 SAUCE
1½ DOZEN OYSTERS, RESERVE
 SHELLS
SLICED TRUFFLES, SAUTÉED

Put shrimp, crabmeat, and flounder through a food chopper using finest blade. Moisten with enough Nantua Sauce to make a spreading consistency. Season to taste with salt and pepper; stir in Tabasco and Worcestershire Sauce. Poach 1½ dozen oysters in their own liquor; reserve. Spread half the Nantua Sauce mixture in 1½ dozen oyster shells; top with a poached oyster and sprinkle each with a few drops of brandy. Cover with remaining sauce and place under broiler until browned. Top each with a slice of sautéed truffle.

YIELD: 3 SERVINGS OF 6 OYSTERS EACH

*See page 95

Château de Mimont

✦ ✦ ✦

BENEDICTINE CODFISH

Morue Fraîche à la Bénédictine

1½ POUNDS CODFISH FILLETS
 1 BOUQUET GARNI
 5 MEDIUM YAMS
 5 TABLESPOONS BUTTER,
 DIVIDED

2 TABLESPOONS LEMON JUICE,
 DIVIDED
1 CUP LIGHT CREAM
½ CUP FINE BUTTERED
 BREAD CRUMBS

Place fillets in a large skillet; add enough salted water to barely cover. Add *bouquet garni*. Cover and simmer 10 minutes or until fish flakes when tested with a fork. Remove carefully; finely flake fish. Cook yams until tender, about 30 minutes. Mash yams with 3 tablespoons of the butter and 1 tablespoon of the lemon juice. Season with salt, pepper, and nutmeg. Beat in cream until fluffy. Add flaked fish to mashed yams, mix well. Spoon into a buttered shallow casserole; sprinkle with crumbs. Bake in a 350°F. oven, 20 minutes, or until crumbs are browned.

YIELD: 6 SERVINGS

Château de Challes

ROAST BASS MUSTARD BERCY SAUCE *Bar Rôti à la Bercy*

1 3- TO 5-POUND DRESSED WHOLE   ¾ CUP MILK
    SEA BASS   3 EGG YOLKS, BEATEN
⅓ CUP MELTED BUTTER   1 TEASPOON SALAD OIL
4 ONIONS   SALT, PEPPER, CURRY POWDER

Sprinkle bass with salt and pepper; place in greased shallow baking dish. Pour melted butter over fish. Bake in a 400° F. oven 12 minutes per pound, or until fish is still moist and flakes easily with a fork. While fish is baking, cut onion into ¼-inch thick slices; separate into rings. Soak in milk 20 minutes; drain. Measure milk; add additional milk to make ¾ cup. Combine with egg yolks and salad oil. Season with salt, pepper, and small amount curry powder. Dip onion rings in batter. Deep-fry at 385°F. 2 minutes, or until golden brown. Transfer cooked fish to serving platter; garnish with parsley and lemon wedges. Sprinkle onion rings over fish. Serve with Mustard Bercy Sauce.*

YIELD: 4 TO 5 SERVINGS

*See page 101

La Cardinale

FILLETS OF SOLE MADAME SPILLMANN
Filets de Sole Madame Spillmann

4 FILLETS OF SOLE   1 TABLESPOON SOUR CREAM
½ CUP WHITE VERMOUTH   1 TABLESPOON HEAVY CREAM
1 TABLESPOON TOMATO PASTE   1 TABLESPOON FINELY SLICED
¼ CUP BUTTER   TRUFFLES

Put sole in large skillet with vermouth, tomato paste, and butter. Cook one minute over high heat then reduce heat until fillets are cooked. Approximately ten minutes. Combine sour and heavy cream. Add cream to sauce, stir. Heat, but do not boil. Place fillets in serving dish. Pour sauce over them and garnish with sliced truffles.

YIELD: 4 SERVINGS

Château d'Artigny

⚜ ⚜ ⚜

FILLETS OF SOLE IN ASPIC

Aspic de Filets de Soles

4 CUPS TOMATO JUICE, DIVIDED
1 BOUQUET GARNI
2 WHOLE CLOVES
6 THIN ONION SLICES
6 PEPPERCORNS, CRUSHED
1 SMALL GARLIC CLOVE
½ TEASPOON SALT
1 ENVELOPE UNFLAVORED GELATIN

6 POACHED FILLETS OF SOLE, CHILLED
6 HARD-COOKED EGGS
COOKED CRAB MEAT
FINELY CHOPPED GREEN PEPPER
FINELY CHOPPED CELERY
CAPERS
SMALL COOKED SHRIMP

Put 3 cups of the tomato juice, *bouquet garni,* whole cloves, onion, peppercorns, garlic, and salt in a saucepan. Bring to a boil; reduce heat and simmer 25 minutes. Strain. Sprinkle gelatin on remaining 1 cup tomato juice to soften. Add to hot tomato juice and stir until dissolved. Chill just until mixture begins to mound. While mixture is chilling, cut each fillet in half and square off. Halve eggs lengthwise; remove yolks. Substitute a small ball of crab meat mixed with mayonnaise and seasoned, for each yolk and adjust the halves together. Put an 8-cup loaf pan into a bed of crushed ice. Pour in a layer of tomato mixture and when almost firm set in the eggs in a row. Cover with a layer of tomato juice and, when almost firm, sprinkle in a thin layer of chopped green pepper. Repeat with tomato then lay in 6 of the sole slices. Top with tomato and alternate tomato layers with a layer of capers and remaining sole slices ending with tomato. Garnish edge of the mold with shrimp. Chill until firm. When ready to serve, unmold onto a chilled platter and garnish with watercress.

YIELD: 6 SERVINGS

Hostellerie de la Poste

✠ ✠ ✠

SALMON STEAK   *Darnes de Saumon*

2 2-POUND SALMON STEAKS
1 BOUQUET GARNI
3 ONION SLICES
1 SMALL CARROT, GRATED
1 GARLIC CLOVE, MASHED
2 WHOLE CLOVES
8 PEPPERCORNS

½ TEASPOON SALT
   MILK
4 EGG YOLKS
1 WHOLE EGG
2 TABLESPOONS LEMON JUICE
½ CUP CHOPPED TOASTED ALMONDS
2 HARD-COOKED EGG YOLKS

Wrap steaks in cheesecloth; secure with a string. Place in a deep kettle with *bouquet garni,* onion, carrot, garlic, whole cloves, peppercorns, and salt. Add enough milk to cover ingredients. Rub top inside edge of kettle with butter to prevent milk from boiling over. Bring to a boil; reduce heat and poach fish 20 to 25 minutes. Lift fish carefully; remove cheesecloth. Transfer to heat-proof platter. Remove center bones; fill with capers. Remove skin. Keep warm. Beat egg yolks and whole egg in top of double boiler over simmering water. Gradually stir in 2 cups of the strained hot milk alternately with lemon juice, until mixture thickens. Stir in almonds; heat. Pour over salmon steaks; sprinkle with sieved hard-cooked egg yolks.

YIELD: 6 TO 8 SERVINGS

Château de la Tortinière

✠ ✠ ✠

BRAISED FRESH SALMON WITH HERBS
Saumon Frais Grillé aux Fines Herbes

¼ CUP OLIVE OIL
¼ TEASPOON WORCESTERSHIRE
    SAUCE
6 SALMON STEAKS, ¾ INCH THICK

1½ TEASPOONS EACH FINELY
    CHOPPED PARSLEY, SHALLOT
    AND CHIVES
    JUICE OF ONE LEMON

Combine olive oil and Worcestershire Sauce. Sprinkle salmon steaks with salt and pepper; dip in olive oil mixture. Broil under moderate heat, 12 minutes on each side, basting occasionally with melted butter. Transfer to a hot platter; remove skin and center bone. Sprinkle with mixture of parsley, shallot, and chives. Add lemon juice to juices in broiler; heat. Pour over salmon.

YIELD: 6 SERVINGS

Château St. Jean

✤ ✤ ✤

CURRY OF SALMON IN RAMEKINS *Saumon à l'Indienne en Casserole*

2 TABLESPOONS BUTTER	1 CUP MILK
2 TABLESPOONS FLOUR	1 CAN (1 POUND) SALMON,
½ TEASPOON SALT	DRAINED AND FLAKED
⅛ TEASPOON PEPPER	1 TEASPOON LEMON JUICE
1 TEASPOON CURRY POWDER	½ CUP BUTTERED BREAD CRUMBS

Melt butter in a saucepan; blend in flour, salt, pepper, and curry powder. Gradually add milk and cook, stirring constantly, until mixture thickens and comes to a boil. Add salmon and lemon juice; heat. Turn into individual casseroles or a 1-quart casserole; sprinkle with buttered crumbs. Bake in a 375°F. oven, 15 to 20 minutes, or until crumbs are browned.

YIELD: 3 SERVINGS

Le Prieuré

✤ ✤ ✤

SALMON SOUFFLÉ *Soufflé de Saumon*

2 TABLESPOONS BUTTER	½ CUP MILK
2 TABLESPOONS FLOUR	4 EGGS, SEPARATED
½ TEASPOON EACH SALT, CELERY	1 CAN (8 OUNCES) SALMON,
SALT, PAPRIKA, AND CURRY	DRAINED AND FLAKED
POWDER	

Melt butter in a saucepan. Blend in flour and seasonings. Gradually add milk and cook, stirring constantly, until mixture thickens and comes to a boil. Remove from heat. Add slightly beaten egg yolks stirring rapidly. Stir in salmon. Beat egg whites until stiff, but not dry; fold into salmon mixture. Turn into a buttered soufflé dish. Bake in a 425°F. oven, 20 to 25 minutes. Serve immediately.

YIELD: 4 SERVINGS

Hostellerie du Prieuré

✦ ✦ ✦

SHAD ROE ROUEN

Laitances d' Alose en Casserole aux Fines Herbes

3 SHAD ROE
1½ CUPS WHITE WINE
1½ CUPS FISH STOCK
1 TEASPOON TARRAGON
   VINEGAR
¼ CUP MELTED BUTTER

1 TEASPOON EACH MINCED
   CHERVIL, PARSLEY, CHIVES,
   AND ONION
⅛ TEASPOON EACH ROSEMARY
   AND MARJORAM
   DASH THYME
¼ CUP SHERRY WINE

Place shad roe in a saucepan; add wine, fish stock, and vinegar. Bring to a boil; reduce heat and simmer 12 minutes. Remove from heat; drain. Pat shad roe dry; roll in olive oil. Place in an earthenware casserole. Bake in a 375°F. oven, 15 minutes, stirring occasionally until browned on all sides. Split in two and return to casserole. Add remaining ingredients. Bake 10 minutes. Serve with potato chips and very thin brown bread and butter sandwiches.

YIELD: 6 SERVINGS

Château de Mercuès

✦ ✦ ✦

CREAMED SHAD ROE IN CASSEROLE

Laitances d'Alose en Casserole à la Crème

3 SHAD ROE
   ANCHOVY BUTTER
1 TEASPOON EACH MINCED PARSLEY,
   SHALLOT, CHERVIL, AND
   MARJORAM

   LIGHT CREAM
1 BAY LEAF
2 ONION SLICES
4 SPRIGS PARSLEY
2 TABLESPOONS BUTTER

Split each roe lengthwise almost to bottom. Spread inside with anchovy butter. Place together and cover each roe with a thin sheet of larding pork. Tie together. Rub with herb mixture. Place in a buttered casserole; sprinkle with freshly ground pepper. Add enough cream to barely cover. Add bay leaf, onion, parsley, and dot with butter. Cover; bake in a 375°F. oven, 25 minutes. Remove cover; bake 5 minutes longer. Remove bay leaf and parsley before serving.

YIELD: 6 SERVINGS

Château St. Jean

❖ ❖ ❖

BAKED SHAD À LA MODE DE NANTES   *Alose à la Mode de Nantes*

2 SHAD ROE	¼ CUP MELTED BUTTER
2 CUPS SOFT BREAD CRUMBS	⅛ TEASPOON NUTMEG
1 CUP CHOPPED COOKED SPINACH	1 4-POUND SHAD, DRESSED
⅓ CUP FINELY CHOPPED CELERY	BRANDY
2 HARD-COOKED EGGS, CHOPPED	SALT AND PEPPER

Simmer shad roe in enough Court Bouillon* to cover, 10 minutes. Chop one roe and cut the other into ⅛-inch thick slices. Combine the chopped roe with remaining ingredients except salt, pepper, and brandy for stuffing. Add salt to taste. Stuff fish; secure edges. Place fish on a large square of buttered brown paper. Rub fish with brandy and sprinkle with salt and pepper. Fold paper over fish; fold ends. Place in a buttered baking pan. Bake in a 375°F. oven, 40 minutes. Open paper and bake 8 to 10 minutes longer, basting with butter. Transfer to serving platter. Dip shad roe slices in melted butter and alternate on top of the shad with thin lemon slices which have been dipped in chopped parsley.

YIELD: 6 SERVINGS

*See page 93

Château de Coudrée

❖ ❖ ❖

BROWN BUTTER SHAD ROE   *Laitances d'Alose au Beurre Noir*

1 SHAD ROE	½ TEASPOON VINEGAR
2 TABLESPOONS BUTTER	1 TEASPOON CAPERS
	1 TEASPOON MINCED PARSLEY

Place roe on greased broiler rack. Broil under moderate heat 10 minutes until golden brown, turning once and brushing frequently with melted butter. Melt butter in a small saucepan and heat until browned; stir in vinegar and salt and freshly ground pepper to taste. Place roe on serving dish; sprinkle with capers and parsley. Pour piping-hot butter over all.

YIELD: 2 SERVINGS

Château de Pilate et Fontager

❦ ❦ ❦

PIKE WITH ANCHOVIES IN MELTED MUSTARD BUTTER

Brochet aux Anchois, Beurre Fondu Moutarde

1 4-POUND PIKE
24 ANCHOVY FILLETS
1 TEASPOON EACH MINCED ONION,
SHALLOT, CHIVES, PARSLEY,
AND CHERVIL

1 GARLIC CLOVE, MASHED
1 TABLESPOON CHOPPED
MUSHROOM
½ CUP WHITE WINE

Trace a line on top of the pike just deep enough to cut the skin. Remove the skin on both sides. Draw anchovy fillets through with a larding needle about 12 to a side. Trim the excess anchovies close to the fish. Have ready a large sheet of buttered brown paper. Combine all remaining ingredients, except wine; season to taste with salt, nutmeg, and cayenne. Sprinkle on paper; place fish on top. Fold paper over fish; fold ends. Place in a shallow greased baking pan. Bake in a 400°F. oven, 12 minutes per pound. Remove paper; transfer to serving platter. Serve with Beurre Fondu Moutarde.*

YIELD: 4 TO 6 SERVINGS

*See page 102

Hostellerie du Prieuré

❦ ❦ ❦

FILLETS OF TURBOT EGGPLANT PARISIAN

Filets de Turbot aux Aubergines

6 TURBOT FILLETS
MILK
FLOUR
1 CUP BUTTER, DIVIDED
1 SMALL EGGPLANT

2 TABLESPOONS LEMON JUICE
1 TABLESPOON MINCED PARSLEY
2 TABLESPOONS BOTTLED THICK
MEAT SAUCE

Dip fillets into milk, then in seasoned flour. Place in shallow baking dish. Melt ⅓ cup of the butter; pour over fish. Bake in a 350°F. oven, 15 minutes, basting occasionally. Cut eggplant into 6 slices; remove skin. Dip in seasoned flour. Melt ⅓ cup of the butter in a skillet. Add eggplant and cook until browned on both sides and tender. Place eggplant on a serving platter; top with turbot fillets and sprinkle with lemon juice and parsley. Melt remaining ⅓ cup butter with meat sauce; pour over fish.

YIELD: 6 SERVINGS

Le Prieuré

❧ ❧ ❧

TURBOT IN CHAMPAGNE

Turbot au Champagne

¼ POUND MUSHROOMS, CHOPPED
2 TEASPOONS MINCED PARSLEY
1 TEASPOON EACH MINCED CHIVES
 AND ONION
½ TEASPOON SALT
1 TABLESPOON FINELY CHOPPED
 SHALLOT

4 TABLESPOONS FISH STOCK
1 5-POUND TURBOT, DRESSED
 CHAMPAGNE
¼ CUP BECHAMEL SAUCE*
¼ CUP BUTTER
¼ CUP SHERRY WINE

Combine mushrooms, parsley, chives, onion, salt, shallot, and fish stock. Place in bottom of a shallow buttered baking dish. Place fish on top. Add enough Champagne to barely cover. Cover and bake in a 400°F. oven, 40 minutes, or until fish flakes easily when tested with a fork. Remove cover; spoon Bechamel Sauce over fish. Bake 5 minutes longer. Transfer to a heat-proof platter; keep warm. Pour sauce into a saucepan; cook until reduced to one-half. Add butter, bit by bit, beating constantly. Stir in wine. Pour over fish. Place under broiler until glazed. *If desired,* garnish with 6 poached egg yolks which have been sprinkled with grated Parmesan cheese and browned under the broiler. Place a spoonful of stewed fresh tomatoes between each egg yolk and sprinkle lightly with minced parsley.

YIELD: 6 SERVINGS

*See page 95

Hostellerie de la Poste

⚜ ⚜ ⚜

STUFFED TROUT IN CHABLIS

Truites Fourrées au Chablis

4 TROUT (½ POUND EACH)
½ CUP BREAD CRUMBS
¼ CUP FINELY CHOPPED
   MUSHROOMS
2 TABLESPOONS SOUR CREAM,
   DIVIDED

2 TABLESPOONS HEAVY CREAM,
   DIVIDED
3 TABLESPOONS CHOPPED
   SHALLOTS, DIVIDED
1 CUP CHABLIS WINE
1 TABLESPOON KNEADED BUTTER
JUICE OF ½ LEMON

Mix together bread crumbs, mushrooms, 1 tablespoon each of the sour cream, heavy cream, and shallots. Have fish dealer clean trout by making opening under the head but leave them uncut otherwise. Force stuffing inside fish. Place individually on buttered brown paper, sprinkle with remaining shallots. Wrap paper; place in buttered baking pan. Add wine. Bake in a 425° oven, 10 to 12 minutes, basting occasionally. Remove fish; keep warm. Strain cooking liquid into saucepan; boil 2 minutes. Blend together remaining sour cream and heavy cream. Add to liquid with kneaded butter and lemon juice. Pour over fish.

YIELD: 4 SERVINGS

Château de Mimont

✦ ✦ ✦

FISH STEW IN RED WINE
La Pauchouse

1 POUND EACH CARP, PERCH, EEL,
WHITING, AND PIKE (OR OTHER
FRESH-WATER FISH)
½ CUP BUTTER, DIVIDED
3 TABLESPOONS CHOPPED ONION
4 GARLIC CLOVES, MASHED

1 BOUQUET GARNI
3 TABLESPOONS BRANDY
CLARET WINE
1 CUP FINELY DICED PORK,
PARBOILED
2 DOZEN TINY WHITE ONIONS

2 DOZEN SMALL MUSHROOM CAPS

Cut fish into 2-inch pieces. Reserve. Melt ¼ cup of the butter in a deep kettle; add onion, garlic, and *bouquet garni*. Cook, stirring occasionally until onion is tender. Flame brandy; pour over fish. Place fish in kettle; add onion mixture and enough claret wine to barely cover. Bring to a boil; cover. Reduce heat and simmer 15 to 20 minutes or until fish is nearly done. While fish is simmering, melt remaining ¼-cup butter in a deep kettle. Add pork, onions, and mushrooms. Simmer 15 to 20 minutes, stirring occasionally. Transfer fish to this mixture. Cover; keep hot. Cook wine-fish stock until reduced to ½ its original volume. Season to taste and thicken if necessary. Strain over fish mixture. Cover; simmer 10 minutes longer.

YIELD: 10 SERVINGS

Château de Trigance

✤ ✤ ✤

FISH STEW PROVENÇALE

La Bourride Provençale

2 POUNDS WHITING
2 POUNDS EEL
1 LARGE ONION, THINLY SLICED
1 SPRIG FENNEL
2 SPRIGS THYME
1 BAY LEAF

2 SPRIGS PARSLEY
1 TEASPOON GRATED ORANGE
  RIND
1 QUART HOT WATER
12 BREAD SLICES
8 EGG YOLKS
AIOLI SAUCE*

Cut fish into 2-inch pieces. Place onion slices in a large skillet; top with fennel, thyme, bay leaf, parsley, and orange rind. Place fish pieces over top; sprinkle with salt and pepper. Add water. Bring to a boil. Reduce heat and simmer 12 minutes, or until fish flakes easily when tested with a fork. Transfer fish to a serving platter; keep warm; strain sauce and reserve. Dampen, but do not soak bread in fish stock; reserve. Beat egg yolks in top of double boiler with 6 tablespoons of the Aioli Sauce. Place over boiling water and add reserved fish stock. Cook, stirring constantly until mixture is the consistency of soft custard. Place bread slices on a serving platter; top with sauce. Serve with fish and pass remaining Aioli Sauce.

YIELD: 6 SERVINGS

*See page 99

Poultry

Château d'Artigny

✢ ✢ ✢

FLAMING CHICKEN

Poulets Flambés Princesse

3 WHOLE 2-POUND BROILER-FRYER
  CHICKENS
  SALT AND PEPPER
3 SMALL ONIONS
  CLOVES
6 THIN CARROT SLICES
3 SMALL CELERY STALKS
9 SPRIGS OF CELERY
1 WHOLE BAY LEAF
  THYME

SAUCE:
½ CUP BUTTER
1 TEASPOON EACH MINCED
  TARRAGON, CHIVES, SHALLOTS,
  PARSLEY, CHERVIL, AND CELERY
  GREENS
¾ POUND THINLY SLICED
  MUSHROOMS
2 TABLESPOONS RUM
2 TABLESPOONS GIN
2 TABLESPOONS YELLOW
  CHARTREUSE
1 LUMP SUGAR

Sprinkle cavity of each chicken lightly with salt and pepper. To each cavity add 1 small onion, stuck with cloves, 2 thin carrot slices, 1 small piece celery, 3 sprigs parsley, ⅓ bay leaf, ⅛ teaspoon thyme. Truss chickens; place on rack in roasting pan. Brush with oil. Roast in a 400°F. oven, 1 hour, 15 minutes. When chickens are done, split in two from the back; discard stuffing. Place on a hot platter; keep warm. In top of a chafing dish at the table, melt butter; add minced herbs and greens; cook 2 to 3 minutes. Add mushrooms and cook, stirring occasionally, 4 to 5 minutes longer. Put rum, gin, and chartreuse into a soup ladle. Dip sugar lump into additional rum; ignite and add to soup ladle. Ladle into the chafing dish until the flame dies. Pour contents of chafing dish over chicken.

YIELD: 6 SERVINGS

Château de Challes

✦ ✦ ✦

CHICKEN CARROT CASSEROLE

Poulet en Casserole Nivernaise

2 BROILER-FRYER CHICKENS, CUT IN
   SERVING PIECES
⅓ CUP BUTTER
⅓ CUP CUBED PORK
1 DOZEN SMALL MUSHROOMS
1 DOZEN SMALL CARROT BALLS

1 DOZEN TINY WHITE ONIONS
1 BOUQUET GARNI
1 GARLIC CLOVE
1½ CUPS WHITE WINE
1 CUP SOUR CREAM
EGG DUMPLINGS

Melt butter in a skillet; add chicken pieces and pork and brown on all sides. Transfer to a deep casserole. Slice mushroom stems; add to casserole with mushroom caps, carrots, onions, *bouquet garni,* and garlic. Pour in wine; season with salt. Cover. Bake in a 350°F. oven, 1 hour. Remove garlic and *bouquet garni.* Place over very low heat and stir in sour cream. Drop egg dumplings by teaspoonful around edge of casserole. Cover and simmer 15 minutes.

YIELD: 8 SERVINGS

EGG DUMPLINGS

Pâtes Cuites aux Oeufs

1 CUP ALL-PURPOSE FLOUR
½ TEASPOON SALT
1½ TEASPOONS BAKING POWDER

1 EGG
1 EGG YOLK
3 TABLESPOONS MILK

Sift together flour, salt and baking powder. Beat together egg, egg yolk, and milk. Stir into flour mixture and blend until smooth.

Hostellerie de la Poste

✦ ✦ ✦

CHICKEN IN BURGUNDY
Poulet au Vieux Bourgogne

1 BROILER-FRYER CHICKEN, CUT IN
  SERVING PIECES
2 CARROTS, SLICED
2 ONIONS, SLICED
½ CUP DICED SALT PORK
2 TABLESPOONS COGNAC
2 TABLESPOONS FLOUR
1 BOTTLE BURGUNDY WINE

2 GARLIC CLOVES, CRUSHED
1 BOUQUET GARNI
½ CUP BUTTER
  SALT AND PEPPER
GARNISH:
½ POUND SMALL WHITE ONIONS,
  PEELED
½ POUND MUSHROOMS
¼ CUP DICED SALT PORK

Brown chicken in butter in skillet with carrots, sliced onions, and ½ cup salt pork. Heat cognac, ignite, pour over chicken. Sprinkle chicken with flour, cook until golden brown. Add wine, *bouquet garni,* and garlic. Bring to a boil and let simmer gently for 45 minutes. Remove chicken; strain sauce.

While chicken is simmering, steam onions with mushrooms and ¼ cup salt pork in butter. Add as garnish to chicken and pour sauce over it.

YIELD: 4 SERVINGS

Château de Pilate et Fontager

✦ ✦ ✦

CHICKEN FRICASSÉE VILLEFRANCHE
Poulet en Fricassée Villefranche

3 DOZEN TINY WHITE ONIONS
2 TABLESPOONS EACH MINCED
  PARSLEY, CHIVES, AND SHALLOT
2 BROILER-FRYER CHICKENS, CUT IN
  SERVING PIECES
  SALT, PEPPER, BAY LEAF, SAGE

¾ CUP OLIVE OIL
2 CANS (4 OUNCES EACH) WHOLE
  MUSHROOMS
1 CUP BROWN SAUCE*

Place half the onions in a large shallow baking pan with cover. Sprinkle with parsley, chives, shallot and season with salt, pepper, crushed bay leaves, and sage. Top with half the chicken pieces. Repeat layers. Pour olive oil over all and add mushrooms with liquid. Cover. Bake in a 350°F. oven, 1 hour. Arrange chicken pieces in a circle on serving platter. Strain onions and mushrooms and place in center. Pour Brown Sauce over vegetables.

YIELD: 8 SERVINGS

*See page 98

Château Choiseul

✦ ✦ ✦

CHICKEN BREASTS IN JACKETS
Poitrine de Volaille Duchesse

½ CUP MAITRE D'HÔTEL BUTTER
6 WHOLE BROILER-FRYER CHICKEN
  BREASTS
  SALT AND PEPPER
  GROUND NUTMEG
  GROUND CLOVES
1 SMALL ONION, FINELY CHOPPED
¾ CUP SLICED MUSHROOM CAPS

3 SHALLOTS, FINELY CHOPPED
4 SPRIGS TARRAGON, CHOPPED
3 CHICKEN LIVERS, GROUND
⅓ CUP GROUND COOKED HAM
1 TEASPOON EACH FINELY CHOPPED
  GREEN PEPPERS AND PARSLEY
6 THIN SLICES BLANCHED
  SWEETBREAD

2 TABLESPOONS CHOPPED TRUFFLES

Melt butter in 2 large skillets. Sprinkle chicken lightly with salt, pepper, nutmeg, and cloves. Brown breasts in butter, about 25 minutes, turning occasionally. Remove. Put all the butter into 1 skillet and add all remaining ingredients except sweetbread slices. Cook until mixture is slightly browned, stirring occasionally. Spread mixture on all sides of chicken breasts. Have ready 6 large squares brown paper. Cut each into the shape of a heart, large enough to enfold chicken. Butter the paper on both sides and place a breast on each, cut side up. Divide remaining mixture on top of the breasts; top each with a sweetbread slice. Bring the two edges together and seal by folding the ends very tight, allowing plenty of room around the breast. Place in a buttered shallow baking pan. Bake in a 350°F. oven, 20 minutes. Place on serving platter, garnish with watercress and broiled tomato halves. Pass Madeira Wine Sauce.* Let each guest unwrap the chicken.

YIELD: 6 SERVINGS

*See page 99

Château de Challes

✠ ✠ ✠

CHICKEN WITH HERB STUFFING
Poulet Bourcey

2 WHOLE BROILER-FRYER CHICKENS
  BRANDY
  SALT AND PEPPER
2 LARGE MUSHROOMS
1 SLICE COOKED HAM
6 PITTED GREEN OLIVES
3 CUPS BREAD CRUMBS
1 TABLESPOON CHOPPED TRUFFLE

1 TEASPOON EACH MINCED
  CHERVIL, CHIVES, AND
  TARRAGON
½ CUP BECHAMEL SAUCE*
½ CUP BUTTER, DIVIDED
1 BOUQUET GARNI
2 CUPS CHAMPAGNE
1 CUP BROWN SAUCE†

Rub cavities of chickens with brandy; sprinkle lightly with salt and pepper. Force mushrooms, ham, and olives through a food chopper. Add to bread crumbs with truffle, chervil, chives, and tarragon. Add Bechamel Sauce; mix well. Stuff chickens; truss. Melt ¼ cup of the butter in a deep kettle. Add one of the chickens and brown well on all sides. Transfer to a large casserole. Melt remaining ¼ cup butter; add second chicken and brown. Place in casserole, add *bouquet garni;* pour in champagne and Brown Sauce. Cover; bake in a 350°F. oven, 40 minutes. Remove chicken to serving platter. Strain sauce over chickens.

YIELD: 8 SERVINGS

*See page 95
†See page 98

Château de Pray

✠ ✠ ✠

CHICKEN ALMOND MOUSSE
Mousse de Volaille Amandine

1 ENVELOPE UNFLAVORED GELATIN
2 CUPS CHICKEN STOCK, DIVIDED
¼ TEASPOON PAPRIKA
  CAYENNE TO TASTE

3 EGG YOLKS, SLIGHTLY BEATEN
⅓ CUP SHERRY WINE
½ CUP GROUND TOASTED ALMONDS
1 CUP GROUND COOKED CHICKEN

1 CUP HEAVY CREAM, WHIPPED

Sprinkle gelatin on ½ cup of the cold chicken stock in top of double boiler to soften. Stir in remaining stock, paprika, cayenne, and egg yolks. Place over hot water and cook, stirring constantly, until gelatin is dissolved and mixture is slightly thickened. Remove from heat; stir in sherry. Chill until mixture begins to mound. Fold in almonds and chicken; fold in whipped cream. Turn into a 6-cup mold; chill until firm. When ready to serve, unmold on serving platter and garnish with watercress.

YIELD: 6 SERVINGS

Château de Pilate et Fontager

✤ ✤ ✤

POACHED CHICKEN SAUCE IVOIRE   *Poulet Poché à la Sauce Ivoire*

1 WHOLE BROILER-FRYER CHICKEN	1 SMALL WHITE TURNIP, DICED
3 APPLE SLICES	1 BOUQUET GARNI
3 ONION SLICES	1 TEASPOON SALT
1 THIN LEMON SLICE	4 PEPPERCORNS
3 CARROTS, CUT IN 1-INCH PIECES	3 TABLESPOONS BUTTER
2 MEDIUM ONIONS, HALVED	3 TABLESPOONS FLOUR
NECK AND GIBLETS	1 CUP HEAVY CREAM

3 EGG YOLKS

Sprinkle chicken cavity lightly with salt and pepper. Add apple and onion slices and lemon; truss. Place in a deep kettle. Surround with carrots, onions, neck and giblets, turnip, *bouquet garni,* salt, and peppercorns; pour in 1 quart water. Bring to a boil. Cover; reduce heat and simmer 1 hour. Remove chicken; keep hot. Prepare sauce by straining stock; measure 1 quart. Melt butter in a deep saucepan; blend in flour. Add chicken stock and cook, stirring constantly, until mixture comes to a boil. Strain into another saucepan. Cook, stirring until mixture is reduced by half. Stir in cream; heat. Remove from heat; beat in egg yolks, one at a time, beating rapidly after each addition. Return to heat; bring just to a boil. Strain into sauceboat. Put chicken on serving platter; discard stuffing. Pass sauce at table.

YIELD: 4 SERVINGS

Le Prieuré

✤ ✤ ✤

CHICKEN IN BURGUNDY WINE

Coquelet Bourguignonne

1 WHOLE BROILER-FRYER CHICKEN, CUT IN SERVING PIECES
1 TEASPOON SALT
⅛ TEASPOON PEPPER
½ CUP BUTTER, DIVIDED
12 SMALL MUSHROOM CAPS
6 TINY WHITE ONIONS
2 OUNCES SALT PORK, FINELY CUBED
1½ CUPS BURGUNDY WINE
1 BOUQUET GARNI
¾ CUP CHICKEN STOCK, DIVIDED
2 TABLESPOONS FLOUR

Sprinkle chicken with salt and pepper. Melt ¼ cup of the butter in a large skillet; add chicken pieces and brown well. Remove. Melt remaining ¼ cup butter in the same skillet; add mushrooms, onions, and salt pork. Cook, stirring occasionally, 5 minutes. Return chicken pieces; pour in wine and add the *bouquet garni*. Bring to a boil. Cover; reduce heat and simmer 45 minutes. Place chicken pieces on serving platter; keep warm. Remove *bouquet garni*. Add ½ cup of the stock to skillet. Blend flour with remaining stock. Cook, stirring constantly, until mixture is slightly thickened. Pour over chicken.

YIELD: 4 SERVINGS

Château d' Ayres

✤ ✤ ✤

SMOTHERED SQUAB WITH GREEN PEAS

Pigeons à l'Etouffade aux Petits Pois

6 1-POUND SQUABS
½ CUP BUTTER
1 MEDIUM ONION, HALVED
1 BOUQUET GARNI
12 ½-INCH CUBES SALT PORK
3 CUPS SHELLED PEAS
¾ CUP CHICKEN STOCK
DASH NUTMEG
½ TEASPOON SUGAR

Sprinkle cavities of squabs lightly with salt and pepper; truss. Melt butter in a large skillet; add squabs and brown on all sides. Place in a large deep casserole. Pour in butter remaining in skillet. Stick cut side of each onion half with a clove and add to casserole; add *bouquet garni* and salt pork. Sprinkle with freshly ground pepper. Cover. Bake in a 300°F. over, 40 minutes. Add remaining ingredients. Cover and bake 40 minutes longer. To serve, remove *bouquet garni*. Place squabs in a circle on serving platter; spoon contents of casserole in center.

YIELD: 6 SERVINGS

Château de Mercuès

✦ ✦ ✦

STUFFED CHICKEN   *Poulet Farci*

2 BROILER-FRYER CHICKENS
4 THIN SLICES VIRGINIA HAM
1 DOZEN OYSTERS
½ CUP CHOPPED, COOKED HAM
3 SHALLOTS, COARSELY CHOPPED
1 MEDIUM ONION, COARSELY
   CHOPPED

2 TABLESPOONS CHOPPED CELERY
   LEAVES
1 GARLIC CLOVE, MASHED
1 BOUQUET GARNI
6 MEDIUM GREEN PEPPERS,
   QUARTERED
1 CUP CHICKEN OR VEAL STOCK

1 CUP SAUTERNE WINE

Have both chickens boned. Place 2 ham slices over cut side of each chicken and top each with 6 oysters. Roll up jelly-roll fashion; secure with string. Place chopped ham, shallots, onion, celery leaves, garlic and *bouquet garni* into a large casserole; place chicken over top. Arrange pepper quarters around chicken. Pour in chicken stock and wine. Cover. Bake in a 350°F. oven, 1 hour. Transfer to serving platter; place green pepper quarters around chicken. Strain remaining ingredients in casserole. Pour half over chicken and pass remaining gravy at table.

YIELD: 4 TO 6 SERVINGS

Château de Trigance

✦ ✦ ✦

RAGOUT OF DUCK ON TOAST   *Salmis de Canard aux Olives sur Toast*

2 TABLESPOONS BUTTER
2 TABLESPOONS FINELY CHOPPED
   COOKED HAM
1 TABLESPOON FINELY CHOPPED
   SHALLOTS OR ONION
3 TABLESPOONS FLOUR
1½ CUPS CHICKEN STOCK

SALT AND PEPPER
THYME
1 TABLESPOON BOTTLED THICK
   MEAT SAUCE
⅓ CUP MADEIRA WINE
3 CUPS COARSELY CUT COOKED
   DUCK

1 DOZEN PITTED RIPE OLIVES

Melt butter in a saucepan. Add ham and shallots and cook, stirring occasionally, 3 to 5 minutes. Blend in flour. Gradually add stock and cook, stirring occasionally, until mixture thickens and comes to a boil. Season to taste with salt, pepper, and powdered thyme. Stir in meat sauce and wine (equal parts of Madeira and port may be used), duck and olives. Heat to serving temperature. Spoon over toast points and serve with guava, currant, or grape jelly.

YIELD: 4 SERVINGS

Château de Betz

✤ ✤ ✤

ROLLED BREAST OF CAPON

Côtelettes de Capon

2 WHOLE BREASTS OF CAPON
6 TABLESPOONS BUTTER, DIVIDED
½ POUND LEAN GROUND VEAL
½ TEASPOON EACH MINCED
    SHALLOT, ONION, CHERVIL,
    PARSLEY, AND TARRAGON

2 TABLESPOONS FINELY GROUND
   MUSHROOMS
½ CUP FINE SOFT BREAD CRUMBS
   MADEIRA WINE
1 EGG BEATEN
½ CUP CHOPPED PISTACHIO NUTS

Have breasts halved, boned, and flattened. Melt 3 tablespoons of the butter in a skillet; add breasts and brown on both sides just until golden. Drain and lay flat. Combine veal, shallot, onion, herbs, and mushrooms. Soak bread crumbs in Madeira; press dry and add. Put through a food chopper twice. Melt remaining butter in a skillet; add stuffing mixture and cook, stirring constantly, over low heat, about 4 minutes. Spread stuffing over chicken breasts; roll up jelly-roll fashion and secure with thread. Roll in beaten egg, then in equal parts of fine bread crumbs and toasted chopped pistachio nuts. Deep-fry at 350°F., 10 minutes, or until golden brown. Serve with hot Madeira Wine Sauce.*

YIELD: 4 SERVINGS

*See page 99

Château de Trigance

✦ ✦ ✦

DUCK IN PORT WINE

Canard au Porto

2 CUPS PORT WINE, SCALDED
½ CUP RAISINS
1 BOUQUET GARNI
¼ CUP CHOPPED GREEN PEPPER
1 GARLIC CLOVE
1 6-POUND DUCKLING
  CALVADOS

⅓ CUP BUTTER
1 TEASPOON SALT
12 PEPPERCORNS
6 ARTICHOKE HEARTS, CUBED
1 CUP BROWN SAUCE*
1 TABLESPOON MINCED PARSLEY

Two days before cooking put scalded wine, raisins, *bouquet garni,* green pepper, and garlic into a porcelain container with tight-fitting cover. Let stand in a cool place, 48 hours, shaking occasionally. Strain. Rub body and cavity of duckling with calvados; truss. Melt butter in a deep kettle. Add duckling and cook until browned on all sides, 15 to 20 minutes, basting with ½ cup of the strained port wine. Pour over remaining port and add remaining ingredients except Brown Sauce and parsley. Cook over low heat 1½ hours. Skim off fat. Remove duckling to serving platter. Add Brown Sauce to kettle and heat; stir in parsley. Pour half the sauce over duckling; pass remaining sauce.

YIELD: 4 SERVINGS

*See page 98

Château St. Jean

✤ ✤ ✤

DUCK IN MADEIRA SAUCE

Canard au Madère

1 5-POUND DUCKLING	1 SMALL ONION, SLICED
1 TEASPOON EACH MINCED CHIVES	½ CUP CHOPPED CELERY LEAVES
AND SHALLOT	1 CUP VEAL STOCK
1 BAY LEAF	½ CUP CIDER
6 SPRIGS PARSLEY	2 EGG YOLKS
2 WHOLE CLOVES	3 TABLESPOONS BUTTER

1 TEASPOON MADEIRA WINE

Mash the duck liver and combine with chives and shallot. Place in cavity and sprinkle cavity with salt, pepper, thyme, and mace. Truss; place in a deep kettle. Add bay leaf, parsley, cloves, onion, celery, veal stock, and cider. Bring to a boil; cover. Reduce heat and simmer 2 hours. Remove duckling; keep warm. Strain the sauce into a saucepan; skim off excess fat. Boil until sauce is reduced to about half its original volume. Add egg yolks, one at a time, beating constantly. Add butter and Madeira; stir until butter is melted. Pour half the sauce over duck; pass remaining sauce.

YIELD: 4 SERVINGS

Hostellerie du Prieuré

✦ ✦ ✦

DUCK AND RICE RING WITH CREAMED SWEETBREADS

Couronne de Canard au Riz à la Normande

CARCASSES OF 2 DUCKLINGS
1 QUART WATER
1 CARROT, QUARTERED
1 MEDIUM ONION, COARSELY
  CHOPPED
2 WHOLE CLOVES
1 BOUQUET GARNI
½ CUP BUTTER

1½ CUPS RAW RICE
½ GARLIC CLOVE, MASHED
1 LARGE ONION, MINCED
1 CAN (20 OUNCES) TOMATOES
¾ TEASPOON SALT
¼ TEASPOON PEPPER
½ CUP SLICED MUSHROOMS
2 CUPS DICED, COOKED DUCK MEAT

Break up carcasses and place in a deep kettle. Add water, carrot, onion, whole cloves and *bouquet garni*. Bring to a boil; cover. Reduce heat and simmer 2 hours. Skim off fat; strain. Melt butter in a large skillet; add rice and cook, stirring occasionally, until yellow. Add garlic, minced onion, tomatoes, salt, and pepper. Bring to a boil; cover. Reduce heat and simmer 15 to 20 minutes, or until rice has absorbed most of the tomato liquid. Add mushrooms and 2 cups of the duck stock. Cover and simmer 10 minutes longer, until rice is tender. Add duck meat; heat 3 to 4 minutes longer. Pack into a buttered ring mold; invert on serving platter. Fill center with Tourte de Ris de Veau filling.*

YIELD: 6 TO 8 SERVINGS

*See page 89

Château de Divonne

✦ ✦ ✦

STUFFED DUCK EN CASSEROLE

Canard Farci en Casserole au Bourgogne

STUFFING:

½ POUND MUSHROOMS, CHOPPED
3 CUPS SOFT BREAD CRUMBS
5 SLICES LIVERWURST
1 TABLESPOON EACH MINCED
   PARSLEY, ONION, CHIVES, AND
   GREEN PEPPER

¼ TEASPOON GRATED LEMON RIND
2 EGGS, BEATEN
   WHITE WINE

Blend together all ingredients except wine. Add enough wine to moisten stuffing.

DUCKLING:

1 5-POUND DUCKLING
   ORANGE JUICE
¼ CUP EACH CHOPPED GREEN
   PEPPER, ONION, CELERY, AND
   TOMATO

½ CUP SLICED MUSHROOMS
1 BOUQUET GARNI
1 GARLIC CLOVE
2 CUPS BURGUNDY WINE
1 CUP BROWN SAUCE*

Rub outside and cavity of duckling with orange juice; sprinkle cavity lightly with salt and pepper. Place in a large casserole with remaining ingredients except Brown Sauce. Cover. Bake in a 350°F. oven, 2 hours. Remove duckling to serving platter; keep warm. Strain contents of casserole into a saucepan; skim off fat. Add Brown Sauce and heat to serving temperature. Pass sauce with duckling.

YIELD: 4 SERVINGS

*See page 98

Château de la Chèvre d'Or

✤ ✤ ✤

DUCK CROQUETTES

Croquettes de Caneton

4 TABLESPOONS BUTTER
2 TABLESPOONS EACH FINELY
   CHOPPED ONION, GREEN
   PEPPER, AND CELERY LEAVES
4 TABLESPOONS FLOUR
1½ CUPS MILK
2 TEASPOONS MINCED PARSLEY

2 CUPS FINELY MINCED COOKED
   DUCK
⅓ CUP FINELY CHOPPED TOASTED
   ALMONDS
SALT, PEPPER, AND MACE
FINE BREAD CRUMBS AND
   FINELY CHOPPED ALMONDS

1 EGG, BEATEN

Melt butter in a saucepan; add onion, green pepper, and celery leaves. Cook, stirring occasionally, until onion is tender. Blend in flour. Gradually add milk and cook, stirring constantly, until mixture thickens and comes to a boil. Remove from heat; stir in parsley, duck, and ⅓ cup almonds. Season to taste with salt, pepper, and mace. Spread on a platter; refrigerate. When ready to serve, form into croquettes. Roll in equal parts of fine bread crumbs and finely chopped toasted almonds; dip in beaten egg and roll in crumb-nut mixture again. Deep-fry at 390°F., 2 minutes. Place in circle on platter; fill center with Mushrooms à la Napolitaine.*

YIELD: 4 SERVINGS

*See page 109

L'Oustau de Baumanière

✤ ✤ ✤

ROAST DUCK IN ORANGE SAUCE
Canard Rôti à l'Orange

4 ORANGES, DIVIDED	SALT, PEPPER, MARJORAM, THYME
1 5-POUND DUCKLING	2 WHOLE CLOVES
¾ CUP WHITE WINE	1 CUP SUGAR
	¾ CUP WATER

Remove orange peel from 2 of the oranges with a vegetable peeler; cut into slivers and reserve. Slice the oranges; place in cavity of duckling and sprinkle lightly with salt, pepper, marjoram, and thyme. Truss; place in a shallow roasting pan; pour in wine. Roast in a 450°F. oven, 15 minutes. Reduce heat to 325°F. and roast 2½ hours. Transfer to serving platter; keep warm. While duckling is roasting, quarter and seed remaining 2 oranges. Combine cloves, sugar, and water in a saucepan. Cook over low heat, stirring constantly until sugar is dissolved. Add orange quarters and boil 5 minutes. Remove quarters; reserve for garnish. Cook the reserved orange peel in boiling water, 5 minutes, drain and chop. Discard water. Strain juices from roasting pan into saucepan; skim off fat. Add rind and bring to a boil. Thicken and season to taste. Pour half the sauce over duckling; pass remaining sauce. Garnish with cooked orange quarters and watercress.

YIELD: 4 SERVINGS

Château d'Ayres

♦ ♦ ♦

ROAST STUFFED DUCK PARMENTIER   *Canard Farci Parmentier*

1 5-POUND DUCKLING	1 TABLESPOON GRATED ORANGE
SHERRY WINE	RIND
SALT AND PEPPER	3 TABLESPOONS MELTED BUTTER
GROUND CLOVES	½ CUP PORT WINE
3 CUPS MASHED POTATOES	½ CUP CHICKEN STOCK
1 CUP CORN MUFFIN CRUMBS	1 BOUQUET GARNI
1 CUP DICED ORANGE SECTIONS	3 TABLESPOONS CURRANT JELLY

Rub outside and cavity of duckling with sherry wine. Sprinkle cavity lightly with salt, pepper, and ground cloves. Combine potatoes, corn muffin crumbs, orange sections and rind; stir in melted butter. Use to stuff duckling; truss. Place in roasting pan; pour in wine and chicken stock; add *bouquet garni*. Roast in a 450°F. oven, 15 minutes. Reduce heat to 325°F. and roast 2½ hours longer, basting frequently. Remove duckling; keep warm. Strain pan juices into a saucepan; let stand a few minutes, then skim off the fat. Add enough chicken stock to make 1 cup. Bring to a boil. Season to taste, then blend in currant jelly. Pass with duckling.

YIELD: 4 SERVINGS

Meats

Château d' Ayres

✠ ✠ ✠

STUFFED LOIN OF VEAL   *Fricandeau de Veau en Daube*

½ POUND LEAN VEAL, GROUND
¼ POUND PORK, GROUND
½ CUP SOFT BREAD CRUMBS
2 TEASPOONS EACH FINELY
   CHOPPED PARSLEY AND ONION
½ TEASPOON GRATED LEMON RIND
1 SLICE GARLIC CLOVE, CHOPPED
1 EGG, SLIGHTLY BEATEN

2 TABLESPOONS SHERRY WINE
1 4-POUND VEAL RUMP ROAST,
   BONED
6 BACON SLICES
2 MEDIUM ONIONS, SLICED
2 CUPS VEAL OR CHICKEN STOCK
1 BOUQUET GARNI
10 PEPPERCORNS

Combine ground veal, pork, bread crumbs, parsley, onion, lemon rind, and garlic in a bowl. Sprinkle lightly with salt, pepper, thyme, cloves, and nutmeg. Stir in egg and sherry. Use to fill cavity of meat; secure opening. Place on a rack in a deep kettle; cover with bacon slices and top with onion slices. Pour in stock; add *bouquet garni* and peppercorns. Bring to a boil. Reduce heat and simmer 2½ hours, or until tender, turning the meat frequently. Do not add more stock. Remove meat, keep warm. Strain gravy into a saucepan. Boil rapidly until reduced to a glaze; use to coat the meat. Place on serving platter and garnish with watercress and gherkins.

YIELD: 6 TO 8 SERVINGS

Château St. Jean

✠ ✠ ✠

FILLET OF VEAL À LA LORRAINE   *Rouelle de Veau Lorraine*

1 3-POUND ROUND VEAL STEAK
1 GARLIC CLOVE
   SALT, PEPPER, MINCED CHIVES

1½ POUNDS FRESH PORK RIND
1½ CUPS WATER
¼ CUP BRANDY

Cut veal into 6 equal portions; lard each portion with strips of pork fat. Rub with a cut clove of garlic and sprinkle both sides lightly with salt, pepper, and chives. Cut pork rind into strips. Place rind and veal in layers in a casserole. Combine water and brandy; pour into casserole. Cover. Bake in a 300°F. oven, 3½ hours. Transfer all of the mixture and juices to a serving platter; sprinkle with equal parts of minced chives and parsley.

YIELD: 6 SERVINGS

Château d'Ayres

✤ ✤ ✤

STUFFED VEAL BIRDS   *Oiseaux sans Tête*

12 VEAL CUTLETS   1½ TEASPOONS SALT, DIVIDED
¼ POUND BACON   ¼ TEASPOON PEPPER
2 GARLIC CLOVES   ⅓ CUP BUTTER
2 TABLESPOONS CHOPPED ONION   1 LARGE ONION, THINLY SLICED
½ POUND SPINACH   1 BOUQUET GARNI
            2 CANS (1 POUND EACH) TOMATOES

Have veal cutlets flattened and sprinkle lightly with salt, pepper, and nutmeg. Force bacon, garlic, chopped onion, and spinach through a food chopper, using finest blade. Stir in 1 teaspoon of the salt and the pepper. Spread mixture on each cutlet. Roll up and tie securely with thread. Melt butter in a deep kettle; add veal and brown on all sides. Add onion and cook until tender. Add remaining ½ teaspoon salt, *bouquet garni,* and tomatoes. Bring to a boil; cover. Reduce heat and simmer 30 to 35 minutes, or until veal is tender.

YIELD: 6 SERVINGS

Château de Betz

✤ ✤ ✤

VEAL BIRDS EN CASSEROLE   *Paupiettes de Veau en Casserole*

6 SLICES VEAL CUTLET   1 CUP WHITE WINE
  SALT, PEPPER, GROUND NUTMEG,   2 DOZEN SMALL MUSHROOMS
  THYME, AND MARJORAM   ¼ CUP DICED GREEN PEPPER
¾ CUP PORK SAUSAGE MEAT   ¼ CUP CHOPPED ONION
4 TABLESPOONS BUTTER   1 BOUQUET GARNI
                                    COOKED SMALL ONIONS

Pound veal very thin, pounding in a mixture of salt, pepper, nutmeg, thyme, and marjoram to taste. Place 2 tablespoons sausage meat on each piece of veal. Roll carefully and tie with thread. Melt butter in a skillet; add veal rolls and brown well. Add wine and bring to a boil scraping up brown particles. Transfer to a 2-quart casserole with cover. Add remaining ingredients except cooked onions. Cover. Bake in a 325°F. oven, 45 minutes. Remove from oven; remove *bouquet garni.* Thicken gravy with a small amount of flour and water. Serve with buttered small white onions.

YIELD: 6 SERVINGS

Château de Challes

♣ ♣ ♣

VEAL KIDNEYS DIJON STYLE   *Rognons de Veau en Casserole Dijonnaise*

6 VEAL KIDNEYS
6 TABLESPOONS BUTTER,
   DIVIDED
1 CUP SLICED MUSHROOMS
¾ CUP LIGHT CREAM

1 TABLESPOON PREPARED MUSTARD
1 TABLESPOON EACH MINCED
   CHIVES, PARSLEY, AND ONION
2 TEASPOONS LEMON JUICE
¼ TEASPOON TABASCO

1 TEASPOON WORCESTERSHIRE SAUCE

Remove membranes from kidneys; cut into slices. Remove fat and veins with scissors. Sprinkle lightly with salt, pepper, and nutmeg. Melt 4 tablespoons of the butter in a skillet; add kidneys and brown quickly on both sides. Transfer to a shallow greased casserole. Melt remaining butter in skillet; add mushrooms and cook, stirring occasionally, until tender. Add to kidneys. Combine remaining ingredients with salt and pepper to taste; pour over casserole. Bake in a 350°F. oven, 15 minutes.

YIELD: 6 SERVINGS

Château de Coudrée

♣ ♣ ♣

VEAL FILLETS TALLYRAND   *Filets de Veau Talleyrand*

1½ POUNDS VEAL CUTLET
 3 TABLESPOONS BUTTER
 ½ CUP LIGHT CREAM
 6 MUSHROOMS, CHOPPED
 2 TEASPOONS FINELY CHOPPED
   SHALLOT

JUICE OF ½ LEMON
1 TEASPOON FINELY CHOPPED
   PARSLEY
2 SLIGHTLY BEATEN EGG YOLKS
HOT MASHED POTATOES

Have veal cutlet cut into 6 pieces and flattened. Melt butter in a skillet; add veal and brown lightly on both sides. Heat cream in another skillet; add veal and keep warm. Add mushrooms and shallot to butter in which veal was cooked; cook 2 to 3 minutes without browning. Transfer butter and vegetables to veal; mix well. Simmer 20 minutes, or until veal is tender. Add lemon juice, parsley, and egg yolks, stirring constantly. Season with salt and pepper. Place veal slices on hot mashed potatoes on serving platter; spoon sauce over top.

YIELD: 6 SERVINGS

Château de la Chèvre d'Or

⚜ ⚜ ⚜

VENETIAN VEAL CUTLETS

Côtelettes de Veau du Doge

6 VEAL CHOPS, ¾-INCH THICK
6 BACON SLICES
2½ CUPS CHICKEN STOCK
1 CUP RAW RICE
1 CAN (6 OUNCES) TOMATO
   PASTE

2 TABLESPOONS BOTTLED THICK
   MEAT SAUCE
6 CANNED ARTICHOKE HEARTS,
   CUBED
6 MUSHROOM CAPS
1 CUP BECHAMEL SAUCE*

2 TABLESPOONS FINELY CHOPPED TRUFFLE

Wipe chops with a cloth dipped in white wine. Season with salt, freshly ground pepper, thyme, cloves, and mace. Place in a greased baking dish; top each with a bacon slice. Bake in a 350°F. oven, 45 minutes or until tender. While chops are baking, bring chicken stock to a boil in a saucepan; gradually add rice. Cover and simmer 20 to 25 minutes, or until all liquid is absorbed. Heat tomato paste with meat sauce; stir into rice mixture with artichoke hearts. Sauté mushroom caps in butter. To serve, pile rice in a mound in center of serving platter. Rest chops against rice to form a crown. Garnish with mushroom caps. Surround base with a ribbon of Bechamel Sauce; sprinkle the sauce with finely chopped parsley alternately with paprika. Add shallots to remaining Bechamel Sauce; pass with veal at table.

YIELD: 6 SERVINGS

*See page 95

Château de Creissels

✦ ✦ ✦

VEAL OLIVES FRENCH METHOD   *Paupiettes de Veau Sauce Brune*

¼ POUND PORK SAUSAGE
¼ POUND GROUND LEAN VEAL
1 TEASPOON EACH MINCED
   PARSLEY, ONION, GREEN PEPPER,
   AND CELERY LEAVES

3 TABLESPOONS BUTTER
6 HAM SLICES
6 THIN VEAL CUTLETS, ABOUT
   1½ POUNDS
2 CUPS BROWN SAUCE*

HOT MASHED POTATOES

Brown sausage in a skillet, breaking up with a fork. Drain off drippings.
Add ground veal, parsley, onion, green pepper, and celery leaves.
Sprinkle with salt and pepper; cook until veal loses its color. Remove
from heat; cool. Place ham slices on veal cutlets; spread cooked mixture
over ham. Roll up; secure with thread. Melt butter in a skillet; add veal
and ham rolls and brown on all sides. Add Brown Sauce. Bring to a boil.
Cover; reduce heat and simmer 1 hour. To serve, place veal and ham
rolls on a bed of mashed potatoes; spoon sauce over all.

YIELD: 6 SERVINGS

*See page 98

Château de Trigance

✦ ✦ ✦

VEAL CHOPS, HERB GRAVY   *Côtes de Veau au Basilic*

6 SHOULDER OR LOIN VEAL CHOPS
2 TABLESPOONS BACON DRIPPINGS
   DASH OF GROUND CLOVES
⅓ CUP FINELY CHOPPED PARSLEY
½ TEASPOON POWDERED BASIL
1½ TEASPOONS GRATED LEMON
   RIND
¾ CUP MEAT STOCK

JUICE OF ONE LEMON
1 LARGE BAY LEAF
1 SLICE GARLIC CLOVE
¼ CUP CHOPPED ONION
3 TABLESPOONS FINELY CHOPPED
   CELERY LEAVES
¼ CUP SHERRY WINE
6 SLICES FRIED TOMATO

Sprinkle chops with salt and pepper. Brown chops on both sides in bacon
drippings in a skillet. Transfer to shallow baking pan. Top with remaining ingredients except sherry wine and tomato. Cover. Bake in a 375°F.
oven, 40 minutes. Place chops on heated serving platter. Stir wine into
gravy. Thicken with a small amount flour mixed with water. Remove
bay leaf. Spoon gravy over chops. Garnish with 6 fried tomato slices.

YIELD: 6 SERVINGS

Château de Pilate et Fontager

✦ ✦ ✦

BRAISED LOIN OF VEAL

Longe de Veau à la Béchamel

1 5-POUND LOIN ROAST OF VEAL
2 CALF'S FEET
1 CUP VEAL TRIMMINGS
¼ POUND SALT PORK, SLICED
1 LARGE CARROT, COARSELY
  CHOPPED
1 LARGE ONION, CHOPPED

½ CUP CHOPPED CELERY AND
  LEAVES
1 BOUQUET GARNI
1 SMALL GARLIC CLOVE
2 WHOLE CLOVES
½ CUP WHITE WINE
1 CUP BEEF STOCK

Put roast into a Dutch oven; add remaining ingredients. Cover. Cook over medium heat about 1 hour, until liquid has evaporated into a glaze, but do not allow to burn. Remove from heat; add enough additional beef stock to bring up to ⅓ the height of meat. Cover; bake in a 350°F. oven, 2 hours, basting occasionally. Remove cover and allow top of meat to brown. Strain gravy. Serve with a sauceboat of gravy and a sauceboat of Bechamel Sauce.*

YIELD: 6 SERVINGS

*See page 95

Hostellerie de la Poste

❖ ❖ ❖

RUMP OF VEAL CONTI

Noix de Veau Conti

1 4-POUND ROUND VEAL STEAK,
  ABOUT 2 INCHES THICK
1 BAY LEAF
¼ TEASPOON EACH THYME AND
  TARRAGON
2 WHOLE CLOVES

1 GARLIC CLOVE
2 MEDIUM ONIONS, QUARTERED
2 CUPS BEEF STOCK
¼ CUP CHAMPAGNE
2 MEDIUM MUSHROOMS, CHOPPED
1½ CUPS BECHAMEL SAUCE*

Lard meat with strips of pork fat. Place in a deep kettle and add bay leaf, herbs, whole cloves, garlic, onions, and beef stock. Bring to a boil. Cover; reduce heat and simmer 1 hour. Remove meat to a roasting pan. Add ½ cup of the strained liquid in which meat was cooked, champagne, and mushrooms. Roast in a 350°F. oven, 2 hours, basting frequently and adding additional strained cooking liquid if necessary. Remove from heat; keep warm. Strain the gravy and measure ½ cup, adding additional strained liquid in which the meat was cooked, if necessary. Stir in Bechamel Sauce; heat but do not boil. Spoon half the sauce on serving platter; top with meat. Spoon several tablespoons of sauce over top of meat; sprinkle with equal parts of finely chopped chervil and parsley. Pass remaining sauce. Serve with Spinach à la Conti.†

YIELD: 6 TO 8 SERVINGS

*See page 95
†See page 115

Château de la Vallée Bleue

✤ ✤ ✤

QUEEN'S VEAL MOUSSE

Mousseline de Veau à la Reine

2 POUNDS VEAL SHOULDER, CUT IN
2-INCH PIECES
1 VEAL KNUCKLE
1 LARGE ONION, SLICED
1 MEDIUM CARROT, QUARTERED

1 BOUQUET GARNI
1 TEASPOON SALT
1 ENVELOPE UNFLAVORED GELATIN
2 EGG YOLKS, BEATEN
½ CUP ICY COLD EVAPORATED
MILK

Put veal into a deep saucepan with knuckle, onion, carrot, *bouquet garni,* salt, and water to cover. Bring to a boil. Cover; reduce heat and simmer 1 hour, 45 minutes, or until veal is tender. Chill in stock; remove chilled fat from stock. Force veal through food chopper, using medium blade. There should be 2 cups. Strain stock; measure 2 cups. Sprinkle gelatin on 1 cup of the stock to soften. Heat remaining stock in top of double boiler. Gradually add a small amount to beaten egg yolks, stirring rapidly. Return to hot stock and cook, stirring constantly, until of custard consistency. Stir in softened gelatin; until gelatin is dissolved. Season with additional salt and pepper if necessary. Cool until mixture mounds. Fold in veal. Whip evaporated milk until stiff peaks form; fold into veal mixture. Turn into a 9 x 5 x 3-inch pan; chill until firm. Unmold to serve. Garnish with salad greens and tomato wedges.

YIELD: 8 SERVINGS

Château St. Jean

✤ ✤ ✤

VEAL CROQUETTE SURPRISE

Croquettes de Veau Surprise

6 HARD-COOKED EGGS
  MELTED BUTTER
  DASH CAYENNE PEPPER
1 TABLESPOON FINELY CHOPPED
  CHIVES
6 PITTED RIPE OLIVES
4 TABLESPOONS BUTTER

4 TABLESPOONS FLOUR
¾ CUP VEAL STOCK
1½ CUPS MINCED COOKED VEAL
1 TEASPOON GRATED ONION
1 TEASPOON MINCED PARSLEY
1 CUP DRY BREAD CRUMBS
¼ CUP GRATED CHEDDAR CHEESE

2 EGGS, SLIGHTLY BEATEN

Halve eggs lengthwise; carefully remove yolks. Mash yolks; add enough melted butter to make a paste. Season with cayenne and blend in chives. Use part of the mixture to stuff olives; place olives in center of 6 of the halves; fill spaces with remaining egg-yolk mixture, spreading enough on the flat white surface to securely top with 6 remaining halves. Melt butter in a saucepan; blend in flour. Gradually add veal stock and cook, stirring constantly, until thickened. Season to taste with salt, pepper, nutmeg, and powdered thyme. Remove from heat; stir in veal, onion, and parsley. Spread out about 1 inch thick on flat platter and chill until firm. When ready to serve, divide chilled mixture into 6 portions. Shape each portion around one stuffed egg. Combine bread crumbs and cheese. Roll veal-coated eggs in crumb mixture, dip in beaten egg, and roll again in crumb mixture. Deep-fry at 390°F., 2 minutes, or until lightly browned. Garnish with deep-fried parsley.

YIELD: 3 SERVINGS

Château de la Tortinière

✦ ✦ ✦

VEAL DUMPLINGS   *Quenelles de Veau à la Béchamel*

2 TABLESPOONS BUTTER	½ CUP VEAL STOCK
4 TABLESPOONS FLOUR	1 POUND BONELESS LEAN VEAL
	2 EGGS

Melt butter in a saucepan; blend in flour. Gradually add veal stock and cook, stirring constantly, until mixture leaves sides of pan and forms a ball. Put veal through a food chopper 3 times, using finest blade. Return to chopper with butter-flour-veal mixture; repeat. Beat in eggs one at a time, beating well after each addition. Force mixture through a sieve. Season with salt, pepper, and a dash of cloves and nutmeg. To form the quenelles, 2 teaspoons are necessary. Dip 1 teaspoon into boiling water and then fill with the quenelle mixture, pressing in the sides. Carefully invert into second teaspoon, which has been dipped in boiling water, and carefully lay in a lightly greased skillet. When all the quenelles are in the skillet, add enough boiling stock or water to barely cover. Bring to a boil; cover. Reduce heat and simmer over very low heat 30 minutes. Remove to serving platter. Spoon 1½ cups Bechamel Sauce* over top.

YIELD: 4 SERVINGS

*See page 95

Château de Cheronnac

✦ ✦ ✦

OVEN-BAKED BEEF

Boeuf à la Mode

MARINADE:

4 POUNDS BEEF ROUND
   SALT, PEPPER, AND GROUND
   NUTMEG
1 SMALL CARROT, SLICED
1 SMALL ONION, SLICED
1 BAY LEAF, CRUSHED

⅛ TEASPOON THYME
2 WHOLE CLOVES
6 PEPPERCORNS
¼ CUP WATER
2 TABLESPOONS TARRAGON
   VINEGAR

1 CUP WHITE WINE

Have beef larded with strips of pork fat. Sprinkle beef lightly with salt, pepper, and nutmeg; place in a deep bowl. Add remaining ingredients for marinade. Cover and marinate in the refrigerator 24 hours, turning occasionally.

TO COOK MEAT:

2 TABLESPOONS BUTTER OR BACON
   DRIPPINGS
   STRAINED MARINADE
2 CALF'S FEET
2 TABLESPOONS BRANDY
2 CUPS RED WINE

1 GARLIC CLOVE, MASHED
1 BAY LEAF
2 SPRIGS PARSLEY
2 CELERY TOPS
1 DOZEN SMALL CARROTS
1 DOZEN TINY WHITE ONIONS

Melt butter in a Dutch oven. Add the meat and sear on all sides until well browned. Add strained marinade, calf's feet, brandy, wine, garlic, bay leaf, parsley, and celery tops. Cover. Bake in a 350°F. oven, 4 hours. Remove the meat and calf's feet to another kettle; strain the gravy over the meat and skim the fat. Add carrots and onions. Cover and return to the oven and bake 1 hour longer.

YIELD: 6 SERVINGS

L'Oustau de Baumanière

❖ ❖ ❖

BEEF TENDERLOIN IN PEPPER SAUCE

Filet de Boeuf Rôti Mariné, Sauce Poivrade

1 WHOLE BEEF FILLET, TRIMMED AND LARDED	¼ CUP OLIVE OIL
1 CUP RED WINE	½ CUP CHOPPED CARROT
¾ CUP TARRAGON VINEGAR, DIVIDED	½ CUP CHOPPED ONION
1 MEDIUM ONION, SLICED	1 BOUQUET GARNI
2 LEMON SLICES	1½ CUPS BROWN SAUCE*
	6 PEPPERCORNS, CRUSHED
	1½ TABLESPOONS BUTTER

Place larded beef filet into a deep casserole. Add wine, ½ cup of the vinegar, onion and lemon slices; cover and marinate in refrigerator 3 days, turning twice a day. Drain, dry, and roast in a 375°F. oven for 1 hour or longer, depending on desired degree of rareness. Baste occasionally. Reserve marinade. Place filet on heat-proof serving platter; cut into portions and reshape as whole roast. Keep warm. Prepare Poivrade Sauce: heat olive oil in a saucepan. Add carrot, chopped onion, and *bouquet garni* and cook until mixture begins to turn color, stirring occasionally. Drain off the oil; discard. Add pan juices, remaining ¼ cup tarragon vinegar, and strained marinade. Boil until mixture is two-thirds its original volume. Stir in Brown Sauce; simmer 30 minutes. Strain into a saucepan; season to taste. Add butter; heat. Pour half the sauce over beef filet; pass remaining sauce at table.

*See page 98

Château de la Chèvre d'Or

✦ ✦ ✦

TENDERLOIN OF BEEF IN CASSEROLE   *Filet de Boeuf des Nautes*

1 WHOLE BEEF FILLET, TRIMMED	½ CUP BUTTER
SALT, PEPPER, THYME, GROUND	1 CUP RED WINE
NUTMEG, AND CRUSHED JUNIPER	1 GARLIC CLOVE
BERRIES	10 PARSLEY SPRIGS
2 MEDIUM ONIONS, SLICED	1 WHOLE ANCHOVY
2 SWEET-SOUR GHERKINS	

Trim tail from fillet; cut remainder into 6 equal portions. Place in a shallow casserole. Sprinkle lightly with salt, pepper, thyme, nutmeg, and crushed juniper berries. Cover with onion slices. Dot with butter; pour in wine. Cover. Bake in a 375°F. oven, 1 hour. Chop garlic, parsley, anchovy, and gherkins. Add to casserole. Cover and bake 30 minutes longer. Remove from oven. Transfer meat to serving platter. If not a sufficient amount of sauce, add beef stock adding 1 tablespoon olive oil for each ½ cup used. Bring to a boil; pour over meat.

YIELD: 6 SERVINGS

Château de la Tortinière

✤ ✤ ✤

BEEF TENDERLOINS IN CRUST
Filet de Boeuf en Chemise

1 3-POUND BEEF FILLET, TRIMMED	PÂTÉ DE FOIE GRAS
COOKED HAM SLICES	CHOPPED TRUFFLES
PUFF PASTE	

Cut tail from fillet. Slice crosswise without cutting all the way through, into 6 equal portions. Spread ham slices on both sides with *pâté de foie gras;* place between slices of beef. Reshape loaf. Roast in a 375°F. oven, 40 minutes. Remove from oven, spread entire fillet with *pâté de foie gras* and sprinkle with chopped truffles. Roll out enough puff paste to cover beef very thin; spread surface with bottled thick meat sauce; place fillet in center and wrap paste around beef. Brush with cold water; place on baking sheet. Bake in a 425°F. oven, 12 to 15 minutes. Brush puff paste with slightly beaten egg yolk and continue baking until browned.

YIELD: 6 SERVINGS

Château de Mimont

✤ ✤ ✤

PARISIAN TONGUE AND SPINACH ROLLS
Bûchettes de Langue de Boeuf

4	POUNDS SPINACH	16	THIN SLICES COOKED TONGUE
1	TEASPOON LEMON RIND	1	CUP SOUR CREAM
3	TABLESPOONS BUTTER	1½	TABLESPOONS HORSERADISH
	SALT, PEPPER, AND GROUND	¼	CUP BREAD CRUMBS
	NUTMEG	¼	CUP GRATED SWISS CHEESE

Wash spinach thoroughly; place in a saucepan without adding water. Add lemon rind. Cover; cook over low heat, 10 minutes, stirring once. Remove from heat; drain. Put through a food chopper, using finest blade. Add butter and salt, pepper, and nutmeg to taste. Heat, but do not boil. Spread the mixture on top of the tongue slices. Roll each up and secure with thread. Place in buttered casserole. Combine sour cream and horseradish; season with salt, white pepper, and a dash of sage. Spoon around tongue rolls. Bake in a 400°F. oven, 15 to 20 minutes. Combine bread crumbs and cheese; sprinkle over casserole. Brown under broiler.

YIELD: 8 SERVINGS

Château de Mercuès

✤ ✤ ✤

MEAT LOAF IN CRUST *Pain de Boeuf Tourangelle*

MEAT LOAF:

2 POUNDS LEAN GROUND BEEF
4 OUNCES CHOPPED SUET
3 EGGS
⅓ CUP SOUR CREAM
1½ CUPS SOFT BREAD CRUMBS

¼ TEASPOON ALLSPICE
2 TEASPOONS SALT
¼ TEASPOON PEPPER
1 TABLESPOON EACH CHOPPED
   SHALLOT, ONION, AND PARSLEY

Combine all ingredients; mix lightly. Pack into a 9 x 5 x 3-inch loaf pan. Bake in a 350°F. oven, 1 hour. Invert and cool 15 minutes.

PASTRY:

PASTRY FOR A 2-CRUST PIE
¼ CUP EACH FINELY CHOPPED
   PARSLEY, ONION, AND GREEN
   PEPPER
⅓ CUP CELERY LEAVES
3 LARGE MUSHROOMS, FINELY
   CHOPPED
4 ANCHOVY FILLETS, CHOPPED

6 RIPE OLIVES, PITTED AND
   CHOPPED
4 PARBOILED CHICKEN LIVERS,
   CHOPPED
⅛ TEASPOON EACH MACE, CLOVES,
   AND PEPPER
½ TEASPOON SALT
2 TABLESPOONS BUTTER

Roll out pastry into an oblong big enough to go around loaf. Combine remaining ingredients; except butter. Moisten with Madeira wine. Cook in butter 5 minutes, stirring occasionally. Cool; spread over pastry. Place meat loaf in center; wrap pastry around meat loaf, sealing edges with water. Cut slits in the top to allow steam to escape; brush with beaten egg yolk. Bake in a 450°F. oven, 10 minutes; reduce heat to 350°F. and bake 15 to 20 minutes longer, or until crust is browned. Remove from oven. Make a small hole in top of the crust. Using a funnel, pour in as much Madeira wine as the loaf will absorb.

YIELD: 8 SERVINGS

Château de Mimont

✣ ✣ ✣

FLANK STEAK CASSEROLE

Flanchet en Casserole

1 3-POUND FLANK STEAK
2 TABLESPOONS FLOUR
1½ TEASPOONS SALT
¼ TEASPOON PEPPER
⅛ TEASPOON GROUND CLOVES
    DASH MACE, CURRY POWDER,
    AND CAYENNE
½ POUND PORK SAUSAGE MEAT
1 CUP SOFT BREAD CRUMBS
¼ CUP MINCED CELERY LEAVES

2 TABLESPOONS EACH MINCED
    PARSLEY AND ONION
1 GARLIC CLOVE, MASHED
1 CAN (3 OR 4 OUNCES) WHOLE
    MUSHROOMS
12 TINY WHITE ONIONS
12 POTATO BALLS
12 CARROT BALLS
6 PEPPERCORNS
1 BOUQUET GARNI

WINE AND BEEF STOCK

Pound steak on both sides with a rolling pin or cleaver while sprinkling with flour, salt, pepper, cloves, mace, curry, and cayenne. Combine sausage, bread crumbs, celery, parsley, onion, and garlic; spread meat with mixture. Roll jelly-roll fashion and secure with string. Brown on all sides in hot fat in a skillet; transfer to a large casserole. Place vegetables in mounds around steak. Add peppercorns and sprinkle lightly with salt. Add *bouquet garni*. Add equal parts of wine and beef stock, slowly so as not to disturb the vegetable mounds. Cover. Bake in a 375°F. oven, 1 hour, 45 minutes. Remove cover and cook 15 minutes longer.

YIELD: 6 SERVINGS

Château de Betz

✦ ✦ ✦

ROAST FRESH MARINATED HAM

Jambon Frais Mariné et Rôti Lorraine

1 7- TO 8-POUND FRESH HAM	¼ TEASPOON EACH POWDERED
3⅛ CUPS WHITE WINE	SAGE, THYME, AND TARRAGON
1 MEDIUM ONION, SLICED	1 GARLIC CLOVE
1 MEDIUM CARROT, SLICED	8 SHALLOTS, MASHED
¼ CUP DICED GREEN PEPPER	12 WHOLE PEPPERCORNS, CRUSHED
12 SPRIGS PARSLEY	2 WHOLE CLOVES, CRUSHED
2 BAY LEAVES	ANCHOVY FILLETS

FINE DRY BREAD CRUMBS

Place ham in a large, deep kettle with a cover; add remaining ingredients except anchovy fillets and bread crumbs. Let marinate in a cool place, 6 hours, turning occasionally. Cover. Bake in marinade in a 375°F. oven, 35 minutes per pound, turning meat every 30 minutes. Remove ham; remove rind. Reserve marinade. Score fat surface, cutting through about ½ inch deep. Insert anchovy fillets into cut areas; sprinkle surface with bread crumbs. Return to oven and bake until golden brown. While ham is baking, strain marinade into saucepan; skim off fat. Boil until mixture is reduced to approximately 1 cup. Season if necessary and pass at table with ham.

YIELD: 14 TO 20 SERVINGS

Le Prieuré

✦ ✦ ✦

HAM MOUSSE

Mousse Chaude de Jambon

2 CUPS DICED, COOKED HAM	1 CUP HEAVY CREAM
2 EGGS, SEPARATED	2 TABLESPOONS SHERRY WINE
SALT, CAYENNE, AND GROUND NUTMEG	

Put ham through a food chopper twice, using finest blade. Beat in egg yolks, add salt, cayenne, and nutmeg to taste. Slightly beat cream and stir in with sherry. Beat egg whites until stiff, but not dry; fold in. Turn into a buttered soufflé dish, filling dish about ¾ full. Bake in a 325°F. oven, 35 minutes, or until firm. Serve with Hollandaise Sauce.*

YIELD: 4 SERVINGS

*See page 99

Château de la Chèvre d'Or

✦ ✦ ✦

ROAST BONED AND STUFFED LEG OF LAMB

Gigot d'Agneau Farci

1 6- TO 7-POUND LEG OF LAMB, BONED FOR STUFFING	1 SMALL WHITE LEEK
¼ CUP SLICED CARROTS	1 BOUQUET GARNI
¼ CUP SLICED WHITE TURNIP	1 CLOVE GARLIC
½ CUP DICED CELERY	1 MEDIUM ONION, SLICED
	1 CUP RED WINE

Prepare stuffing. Stuff lamb; sew or skewer together. Place in a shallow roasting pan. Add remaining ingredients. Roast in a 450°F. oven, 25 minutes. Reduce heat to 350°F. and roast 2 hours longer. Remove roast from pan. Strain gravy in pan into saucepan. Thicken with small amount of flour mixed with water.

STUFFING:

½ CUP CHOPPED, COOKED HAM	1 TABLESPOON FINELY CHOPPED CELERY LEAVES
2 OUNCES GROUND SUET	3 COOKED CHICKEN LIVERS, CHOPPED
6 SLICES DAY-OLD BREAD, CRUMBED	
2 TABLESPOONS CHOPPED ONION	1 TEASPOON SALT
1 TABLESPOON FINELY CHOPPED GREEN PEPPER	¼ TEASPOON PEPPER
1 TABLESPOON FINELY CHOPPED PARSLEY	⅛ TEASPOON NUTMEG

COMBINE ALL INGREDIENTS.

Château d'Ayres

✤ ✤ ✤

BAKED LAMB CHOPS IN WINE

Côtes d'Agneau au Laurier

6 SHOULDER LAMB CHOPS
3 TABLESPOONS BUTTER
2 TABLESPOONS FLOUR
1 CUP WHITE WINE
½ CUP WATER
3 BAY LEAVES

1 BOUQUET GARNI
12 TINY WHITE ONIONS
12 SMALL MUSHROOM CAPS
12 TINY CARROT BALLS
SMALL BOILED WHOLE POTATOES
MINT JELLY

Sprinkle lamb chops with salt and pepper. Brown on both sides in butter in skillet; transfer to shallow baking pan. Blend flour into butter mixture scraping up all brown particles and brown lightly. Add wine and water and cook, stirring constantly, until mixture thickens and comes to a boil. Add remaining ingredients; pour over lamb chops. Cover. Bake in a 375°F. oven, 30 minutes. Season to taste; remove bay leaves and *bouquet garni*. Serve with small boiled whole potatoes and mint jelly.

YIELD: 6 SERVINGS

Château St. Jean

✤ ✤ ✤

BRAISED LIVER FRENCH STYLE

Foie Braisé à la Française

1 2-POUND PIECE BEEF OR PORK
   LIVER
   SALT, PEPPER, SAGE, THYME, AND
   ALLSPICE
3 TABLESPOONS BUTTER
2 CUPS HOT BEEF STOCK
3 SPRIGS PARSLEY

1 BAY LEAF
2 WHOLE CLOVES
1 SMALL GARLIC CLOVE
12 TINY WHITE ONIONS
8 MUSHROOMS
1 CUP DIAGONALLY SLICED
   CELERY

2 TABLESPOONS SHERRY WINE

Sprinkle liver lightly with salt, pepper, sage, thyme, and allspice. Melt butter in a skillet; add liver and brown on both sides. Remove to shallow baking pan. Add remaining ingredients; cover. Bake in a 350°F. oven, 1½ hours. Transfer liver to serving platter; surround with vegetables. Strain gravy and thicken with a little flour; pour over the liver. Sprinkle with minced parsley.

YIELD: 6 TO 8 SERVINGS

Château de Pilate et Fontager

✤ ✤ ✤

INDIVIDUAL MUTTON PIES
Tourtes de Mouton à la Toulousaine

2 POUNDS BONED SHOULDER
OF MUTTON
⅓ CUP BUTTER
1 MEDIUM ONION, SLICED
3 CUPS RED WINE
2 LARGE TOMATOES, PEELED
AND QUARTERED

3 LARGE MUSHROOMS, SLICED
2 CUPS SHELLED FRESH LIMA BEANS
1 BOUQUET GARNI
6 PEPPERCORNS
2 TABLESPOONS FINELY CHOPPED
CHIVES
GARLIC SAUSAGE SLICES

PASTRY FOR 1-CRUST PIE

Cut mutton into 1-inch pieces; roll in seasoned flour. Melt butter in a deep kettle; add onion and cook until tender. Remove onion. Add mutton and cook until browned on all sides. Return onion and add wine, mushrooms, tomatoes, lima beans, *bouquet garni,* and peppercorns. Bring to a boil. Cover; reduce heat and simmer 2 hours, or until mutton is tender. Transfer to a large casserole; sprinkle with chives and cover with sliced garlic sausage. Roll out pastry; cover casserole and secure edges. Cut slits in pastry to allow steam to escape. Bake in a 425°F. oven, 15 to 20 minutes, or until browned.

YIELD: 6 SERVINGS

Château de la Vallée Bleue

✣ ✣ ✣

BROILED LIVER BÉARNAISE

Foie Grillé Béarnaise

3 TABLESPOONS FINELY CHOPPED ONION	3 EGG YOLKS
2 TABLESPOONS TARRAGON VINEGAR	2 TABLESPOONS CHOPPED PARSLEY
	1 TABLESPOON CHOPPED PICKLE
	2 POUNDS VEAL OR CALVES' LIVER

4 TABLESPOONS BACON DRIPPINGS

Put onion and vinegar in top of a double boiler over direct heat. Cook until onion is tender, about 5 minutes. Place over hot water. Add egg yolks one at a time, beating rapidly. Cook until creamy. Remove from water; stir in chopped parsley, pickle, salt, and cayenne to taste. Keep warm. Cut liver into ¼-inch thick slices. Dip slices in seasoned flour. Heat bacon drippings in a large skillet; add liver, cook quickly until browned on both sides, turning once, about 5 minutes. Serve with reserved sauce.

YIELD: 6 TO 8 SERVINGS

Château de Divonne

✣ ✣ ✣

BROILED VEAL KIDNEYS IN SAUCE

Rognons de Veau Grillés Chantecler

6 VEAL KIDNEYS	1 SMALL BAY LEAF
¾ CUP RED WINE	DASH POWDERED BASIL, THYME, AND MACE
3 TABLESPOONS OLIVE OIL	
1 TEASPOON EACH MINCED CHIVES, PARSLEY, ONION, AND SHALLOT	4 TABLESPOONS CURRANT JELLY
1 SMALL GARLIC CLOVE, MASHED	1 TEASPOON PREPARED HORSERADISH

1 TABLESPOON BUTTER

Remove outer membrane from kidneys; halve, but do not separate. Remove fat and veins with scissors. Wash and pat dry. Place in a deep bowl. Combine remaining ingredients except jelly, horseradish, and butter; add to kidneys. Season to taste with salt and pepper. Marinate 1 hour, turning occasionally. Remove from marinade; strain. Dip kidneys into strained marinade; roll in fine bread crumbs. Broil 3 inches from heat, 5 to 7 minutes on each side. While kidneys are broiling, put marinade into a saucepan with jelly and horseradish. Bring to a boil; stir in butter. Put kidneys on toast; pour part of the sauce over kidneys. Garnish with watercress; pass remaining sauce at table.

YIELD: 6 SERVINGS

Château Choiseul

✤ ✤ ✤

SWEETBREADS IN WHITE WINE
Ris de Veau au Vin Blanc

3 PAIRS VEAL SWEETBREADS
WATER
WHITE WINE
2 TABLESPOONS EACH MINCED
PARSLEY, CHERVIL, CHIVES,
MUSHROOMS, SHALLOTS, AND
TRUFFLES
1 GARLIC CLOVE, MASHED
½ CUP BUTTER

6 THIN SLICES HAM
12 MUSHROOM CAPS
2 DOZEN TINY WHITE ONIONS
2 BAY LEAVES
3 SPRIGS PARSLEY
8 PEPPERCORNS
1 CUP WHITE WINE OR
CHAMPAGNE
1 CUP CHICKEN STOCK

Put sweetbreads into a saucepan with equal parts of water and white wine to cover. Bring to a boil; reduce heat and simmer 30 minutes. Remove sweetbreads; place under running water and slip off membrane. Remove veins and connective tissue. Cut sweetbreads into 3 lengthwise slices. Blend together minced parsley, chervil, chives, mushrooms, shallots, truffles, garlic, and butter; spread over sweetbread slices. Reform sweetbreads into their original shape; wrap ham around each and secure with thread. Place in bottom of a deep casserole with tight-fitting cover. Add mushrooms, onions (2 of which have been studded with whole cloves), and remaining ingredients. Cover, bake in a 375°F. oven, 40 minutes. To serve, place sweetbreads in a circle on serving platter. Remove cloves from onions and pile onions and mushrooms in the center; keep warm. Strain sauce into a saucepan and boil rapidly until reduced to 1 cup. Pour over sweetbreads and garnish with buttered toast triangles.

YIELD: 6 SERVINGS

Hostellerie du Prieuré

✦ ✦ ✦

SWEETBREAD PIE *Tourte de Ris de Veau*

ALMOND BUTTER CRUST:

1⅓ CUPS SIFTED ALL-PURPOSE
  FLOUR
½ TEASPOON SALT
¼ TEASPOON BAKING POWDER
½ CUP BUTTER

1 TABLESPOON TARRAGON
  VINEGAR
2 TABLESPOONS COLD WATER
⅓ CUP FINELY CHOPPED BLANCHED
  ALMONDS

Sift together flour, salt, and baking powder into a bowl. Cut in butter until mixture resembles coarse meal. Combine tarragon vinegar and water. Add a tablespoon at a time and stir until mixture forms a ball. Cover and chill. Reserve almonds.

FILLING:

2 PAIRS SWEETBREADS
  WATER
  WHITE WINE
1 BOUQUET GARNI
1 TEASPOON SALT
6 PEPPERCORNS
1 GARLIC CLOVE
4 MEDIUM ONIONS
1 CUP HEAVY CREAM
1 CAN (3 OR 4 OUNCES) WHOLE
  MUSHROOMS

2 HARD-COOKED EGG WHITES,
  CHOPPED
1 CANNED PIMENTO
2 TABLESPOONS CHOPPED GREEN
  PEPPER
2 TABLESPOONS EACH MINCED
  PARSLEY AND CHIVES
3 TABLESPOONS CAPERS
1 TRUFFLE, THINLY SLICED
2 TABLESPOONS MADEIRA WINE

Put sweetbreads into a deep saucepan. Add equal parts of water and white wine to cover. Add *bouquet garni,* salt, peppercorns, and garlic. Stick onions with whole cloves; add. Bring to a boil; reduce heat and simmer 30 minutes. Remove sweetbreads. Place under running water and slip off membrane. Remove veins and connective tissue. Dice sweetbreads; reserve. Remove onions, *bouquet garni,* and garlic from stock; discard whole cloves. Mash onions and return to stock. Boil until liquid is reduced to 1 cup. Add cream; heat. Add diced sweetbreads and remaining ingredients. Heat, but do not boil. Turn into a large casserole. Roll out the almond butter crust ⅛-inch thick. Sprinkle with reserved almonds and press in with rolling pin. Arrange over casserole; flute edges. Cut several slits in crust to allow steam to escape. Bake in a 450°F. oven, 10 minutes. Reduce to 350°F. and bake 25 to 30 minutes longer.

YIELD: 4 SERVINGS

Sauces

WHITE WINE COURT BOUILLON *Court Bouillon au Vin Blanc*

1 QUART DRY WHITE WINE
1 QUART COLD WATER
1 TABLESPOON SALT
2 CARROTS, SLICED
2 MEDIUM ONIONS, SLICED
1 BOUQUET GARNI
12 PEPPERCORNS, CRUSHED

Put all ingredients into a deep kettle. Bring to a boil; reduce heat. Add desired fish or poultry and simmer until tender, depending on size and type of fish or poultry. Strain stock; chill and reserve. Use to cook additional fish or poultry.

YIELD: APPROXIMATELY 2 QUARTS

✤ ✤ ✤

ANCHOVY CRUMB PASTE *Sauce aux Anchois*

¼ CUP BUTTER
1¾ CUPS FINE BREAD CRUMBS
¼ CUP OLIVE OIL
1 MEDIUM ONION, MINCED
2 SPRIGS FENNEL, MINCED
10 ANCHOVY FILLETS, CHOPPED

Melt butter in a saucepan; add crumbs and cook, stirring occasionally, until crumbs are lightly browned. Heat olive oil in another saucepan; add onion and cook until tender and browned. Add to crumb mixture with fennel and anchovies. Let simmer 5 minutes. Serve with hot cooked macaroni, noodles, or spaghetti.

YIELD: APPROXIMATELY 2½ CUPS

✤ ✤ ✤

ANCHOVY MUSTARD SAUCE *Sauce Moutarde aux Anchois*

¾ CUP OLIVE OIL
2 TABLESPOONS PREPARED
   MUSTARD
1 SMALL GARLIC CLOVE, HALVED
1 TABLESPOON MINCED PARSLEY
4 ANCHOVY FILLETS, FINELY
   CHOPPED
½ TEASPOON SUGAR
DASH CAYENNE
1 TEASPOON EACH GRATED ONION,
   CHIVES, AND CHERVIL
2 HARD-COOKED EGGS, FINELY
   CHOPPED
2 TABLESPOONS TARRAGON VINEGAR OR LEMON JUICE

Put all ingredients in a large mixing bowl; beat well 3 or 4 minutes. Add 4 ice cubes; beat from bottom of mixing bowl with a fork. Sauce will thicken immediately. Discard ice and garlic.

YIELD: APPROXIMATELY 1 CUP

MUSTARD SAUCE

Sauce Moutarde

DASH SALT
2 TABLESPOONS FLOUR
¾ TEASPOON SUGAR

2 TEASPOONS PREPARED MUSTARD
¾ CUP MEAT OR CHICKEN STOCK
2 EGG YOLKS, SLIGHTLY BEATEN

Blend together salt, flour, and sugar in top of double boiler. Stir in mustard and stock. Place over hot water, stirring constantly, until mixture thickens. Remove from heat; add egg yolks, beating rapidly. Return to heat and cook, stirring constantly, until mixture is slightly thickened. Serve with smoked meat, corned beef, boiled beef or pork.

YIELD: APPROXIMATELY 1 CUP

Note: If sauce is to be served with fish, substitute fish stock for meat stock and add 2 tablespoons vinegar.

ESSENCE OF MUSHROOMS

Essence de Champignons

1 POUND MUSHROOMS
¼ CUP COARSE SALT
1 BOUQUET GARNI

12 PEPPERCORNS
2 OR 3 SPRIGS FRESH OR DRIED
DILL

Put mushrooms into an earthenware vessel; sprinkle with salt. Cover with several thicknesses cheesecloth. Let stand 15 hours in a cool place. Drain without pressing and force mushrooms through a food chopper using finest blade. Place a bowl under the chopper to retain the juices. Put the juice into a saucepan; add *bouquet garni,* peppercorns, and dill. Simmer 15 minutes. Strain into sterilized jars; seal. Store in a cool place.

EGG SAUCE PARISIAN METHOD

Sauce aux Oeufs Parisienne

1 TABLESPOON SWEET BUTTER, OR
2 TABLESPOONS OLIVE OIL
2 EGGS SEPARATED

2 TEASPOONS TARRAGON VINEGAR
1 HARD-COOKED EGG, COARSELY
CHOPPED

1 TEASPOON MINCED CHERVIL

Melt butter or heat olive oil in top of double boiler over hot, not boiling water. Beat together egg yolks and tarragon vinegar. Add to double boiler, stirring rapidly. Cook, stirring constantly, until it reaches the consistency of heavy cream. Remove from water. Season to taste with salt, pepper, and nutmeg. Beat egg whites. Fold into yolk mixture alternately with chopped egg and chervil.

YIELD: APPROXIMATELY ½ CUP

MARINIÈRE SAUCE

Sauce Marinière

2 TABLESPOONS BUTTER
2 TABLESPOONS MINCED SHALLOTS
1 CUP WHITE WINE
½ CUP FISH STOCK
½ CUP MUSSEL LIQUOR

3 EGG YOLKS, SLIGHTLY BEATEN
4 TABLESPOONS BUTTER
1½ TABLESPOONS LEMON JUICE
1 TEASPOON FINELY CHOPPED
PARSLEY

Melt butter in a saucepan; add shallots and cook until golden brown. Add wine and fish stock and cook until mixture is reduced to two-thirds. Add mussel liquor combined with egg yolks, stirring rapidly. Simmer 5 minutes. When ready to serve, gradually add butter alternately with lemon juice. Stir in chopped parsley. Serve with white fish.

YIELD: APPROXIMATELY 1½ CUPS

BÉCHAMEL SAUCE

Sauce Béchamel

¼ POUND VEAL
6 TABLESPOONS BUTTER, DIVIDED
¼ TEASPOON POWDERED THYME
⅛ TEASPOON WHITE PEPPER

DASH GROUND NUTMEG
¼ CUP FINELY CHOPPED ONION
4 TABLESPOONS FLOUR
1 QUART MILK

Cut veal into small pieces. Melt 2 tablespoons of the butter in a saucepan. Add veal, thyme, pepper, and nutmeg. Cook until veal is heated through, but do not brown. Remove from heat. Melt remaining 4 tablespoons butter in top of double boiler over direct heat. Add onion and cook until tender, but not brown. Blend in flour. Gradually add milk and cook, stirring constantly, until mixture thickens and comes to a boil. Add veal mixture. Place over hot water and simmer 30 minutes, stirring occasionally. Strain.

YIELD: APPROXIMATELY 1 QUART

NANTUA SAUCE

Sauce Nantua

1 CUP BECHAMEL SAUCE*
¼ CUP HEAVY CREAM

2 TABLESPOONS SHRIMP OR
CRAYFISH BUTTER

Combine Bechamel Sauce and cream in a saucepan. Heat, but do not boil. Stir in shrimp butter.

YIELD: APPROXIMATELY 1¼ CUPS

* See above.

PROVENÇALE SAUCE

Sauce Provençale

1 DOZEN MEDIUM TOMATOES
½ CUP OLIVE OIL
¼ TEASPOON SUGAR
1 LARGE GARLIC CLOVE, MASHED
2 TEASPOONS MINCED PARSLEY

Peel tomatoes; remove seeds; quarter. Heat olive oil in a deep saucepan; add tomatoes, salt and pepper to taste, sugar, garlic, and parsley. Simmer 20 to 30 minutes.

YIELD: APPROXIMATELY 1 QUART

✢ ✢ ✢

SUPREME SAUCE

Sauce Suprême

3 TABLESPOONS BUTTER
3 TABLESPOONS FLOUR
1 CUP CONCENTRATED CHICKEN
STOCK*
⅓ CUP HEAVY CREAM
2 EGG YOLKS, BEATEN
3 TABLESPOONS SHERRY WINE
1½ TABLESPOONS FINELY CHOPPED
TRUFFLE
½ TEASPOON PAPRIKA
2 TEASPOONS LEMON JUICE

Melt butter in a saucepan; blend in flour. Gradually add chicken stock and cook, stirring constantly, until mixture thickens and comes to a boil. Remove from heat. Mix together cream and egg yolks; add to sauce, stirring rapidly. Stir in sherry. Return to heat and bring just to a boil. Remove, season with salt and pepper, and stir in remaining ingredients.

YIELD: APPROXIMATELY 1½ CUPS

*To obtain concentrated chicken stock, boil 2 cups chicken stock until reduced to 1 cup.

✢ ✢ ✢

TOMATO SAUCE

Sauce Tomate

1 CAN (1 POUND) TOMATOES
1 TABLESPOON FINELY CHOPPED
ONION
½ GARLIC CLOVE, PEELED
5 PEPPERCORNS, CRUSHED
1 TEASPOON SUGAR
1 BOUQUET GARNI
1 TABLESPOON BUTTER
2 TEASPOONS FLOUR

Put tomatoes, onion, garlic, peppercorns, sugar, and *bouquet garni* into a saucepan. Bring to a boil. Reduce heat and simmer 30 minutes, stirring occasionally. Strain; return strained sauce to saucepan. Place over low heat. Blend together butter and flour. Gradually add to sauce, stirring constantly, until sauce is slightly thickened.

YIELD: APPROXIMATELY 1¾ CUPS

BÉARNAISE SAUCE

Sauce Béarnaise

½ CUP WHITE WINE
½ TEASPOON TARRAGON VINEGAR
1 SPRIG PARSLEY
½ TEASPOON DRIED TARRAGON
1 TABLESPOON FINELY CHOPPED
⅓ CUP BOILING WATER

SHALLOTS
2 PEPPERCORNS, CRUSHED
¼ TEASPOON SALT
½ CUP BUTTER
2 EGG YOLKS

Put wine, vinegar, parsley, tarragon, shallots, peppercorns, and salt into a saucepan. Cook until mixture is reduced to 3 tablespoons. Strain; cool. Put ⅓ of the butter, egg yolks, and cooled tarragon mixture in top of double boiler. Place over hot water, stirring constantly, until butter is melted. Add second portion butter and stir constantly until butter is melted. Repeat with third portion, stirring constantly. Slowly pour in boiling water, stirring briskly. Cook 1 minute longer; remove from heat. Serve with broiled fish or steak.

YIELD: APPROXIMATELY 1 CUP

Note: If sauce curdles, add 2 tablespoons heavy cream or 2 tablespoons boiling water, pouring very slowly and beating briskly.

SOUR CREAM WINE SAUCE

Sauce Smitane

1½ TABLESPOONS BUTTER
2 SMALL ONIONS, FINELY CHOPPED

½ CUP WHITE WINE
1 CUP SOUR CREAM, SCALDED

Melt butter in a saucepan; add onion and cook until tender. Add wine and cook until mixture is reduced almost completely. Add sour cream; simmer 5 minutes. Strain through cheesecloth; then season with salt and pepper to taste and add a small amount lemon juice, if desired. Serve with game.

YIELD: APPROXIMATELY 1 CUP

DEMI-GLACE SAUCE

Sauce Demi-Glace

1 CUP BROWN SAUCE*
4 TABLESPOONS TOMATO PURÉE

½ CUP WHITE WINE

Put Brown Sauce in saucepan. Add white wine and tomato purée. Bring to a boil and allow to reduce to half volume over high heat. Season to taste with salt and pepper.

YIELD: 1¾ CUPS

*See page 98

SAUCE ROBERT

Sauce Robert

2 TABLESPOONS BUTTER
1 LARGE ONION, FINELY
  CHOPPED
1½ CUPS WHITE WINE

1 CUP DEMI-GLACE SAUCE*
⅛ TEASPOON SUGAR
1 TABLESPOON PREPARED
  MUSTARD

Melt butter in a saucepan; add onion and cook until tender. Add wine and cook until mixture is reduced to two-thirds. Add Demi-Glace and simmer 15 minutes, stirring occasionally. Season to taste with salt and pepper and add sugar and mustard. Strain. Do not allow to boil after mustard has been added.

YIELD: APPROXIMATELY 1½ CUPS

*See page 97

✤ ✤ ✤

SAUCE LYONNAISE

Sauce Lyonnaise

3 TABLESPOONS BUTTER
3 MEDIUM ONIONS, FINELY
  CHOPPED

½ CUP WHITE WINE
½ CUP WINE VINEGAR
1½ CUPS DEMI-GLACE SAUCE*

Melt butter in a saucepan. Add onion and cook until tender, but not brown. Add wine and wine vinegar. Cook until mixture is reduced to two-thirds its original volume, stirring occasionally. Add Demi-Glace Sauce; simmer 15 minutes. Strain through a fine sieve; season to taste.

YIELD: APPROXIMATELY 2 CUPS

*See page 97

✤ ✤ ✤

BROWN SAUCE

Sauce Brune

2 TABLESPOONS BUTTER
1 MEDIUM CARROT
1 MEDIUM ONION
2 SPRIGS PARSLEY
1 BAY LEAF

2 TABLESPOONS FLOUR
1 CUP WHITE WINE
1½ CUPS BEEF STOCK
½ TEASPOON SALT
⅛ TEASPOON PEPPER

Melt butter in a saucepan. Add carrot, onion, parsley, and bay leaf and cook until vegetables are lightly browned. Blend in flour; cook until lightly browned. Add wine, stock, salt, and pepper. Bring to a boil. Cover; reduce heat and simmer 30 minutes. Strain.

YIELD: APPROXIMATELY 2¼ CUPS

HOLLANDAISE SAUCE

Sauce Hollandaise

½ CUP BUTTER
2 EGG YOLKS
2 TABLESPOONS LEMON JUICE

¼ TEASPOON DRY MUSTARD
¼ TEASPOON SALT
DASH CAYENNE PEPPER

⅓ CUP BOILING WATER

Put ⅓ of the butter, egg yolks, and lemon juice in top of a double boiler. Place over hot water, stirring constantly until butter is melted. Add second portion of butter and stir constantly until butter is melted. Repeat with third portion, stirring constantly. Add dry mustard, salt, and cayenne. Slowly pour in boiling water, stirring briskly. Cook one minute longer; remove from heat. Serve with white fish, asparagus, cauliflower, or broccoli.

YIELD: APPROXIMATELY 1 CUP

Note: If sauce curdles, add 2 tablespoons heavy cream or 2 tablespoons boiling water, pouring very slowly and beating briskly.

⚜ ⚜ ⚜

MADEIRA WINE SAUCE

Sauce au Madère

1½ CUPS DEMI-GLACE SAUCE*   ¼ CUP MADEIRA WINE

Pour sauce into a saucepan. Cook over medium heat, stirring occasionally, until reduced to ¾ cup. Stir in Madeira, heat.

YIELD: 1 CUP

*See page 97

⚜ ⚜ ⚜

AIOLI

Aioli

2 TO 3 GARLIC CLOVES, PEELED
2 EGG YOLKS
1 CUP OLIVE OIL
1 TEASPOON LEMON JUICE OR

TARRAGON VINEGAR
ICE-COLD WATER
SALT
PEPPER

Pound garlic cloves with egg yolks until blended and smooth. Add olive oil, drop by drop, and as sauce begins to thicken, gradually pour in oil in a thin stream. When half the oil has been incorporated, alternate with lemon juice and ice-cold water. Season to taste with salt and pepper. Serve with cold meat, fish, or vegetables.

YIELD: APPROXIMATELY 1¼ CUPS

DEVILED SAUCE

Sauce Diable

½ CUP TARRAGON VINEGAR
2 SMALL GARLIC CLOVES
1 TEASPOON DRY MUSTARD
2 SMALL BAY LEAVES
¾ TEASPOON SALT
1 TEASPOON PAPRIKA
  DASH CAYENNE

12 PEPPERCORNS
1 CUP TOMATO SAUCE
1 TEASPOON BOTTLED THICK
  MEAT SAUCE
¼ CUP BEEF BOUILLON
½ TEASPOON WORCESTERSHIRE
  SAUCE

1 TABLESPOON BUTTER

Combine vinegar, garlic, mustard, bay leaves, salt, paprika, cayenne, and peppercorns in a saucepan. Bring to a boil. Cook until mixture is reduced to one-half. Strain into a saucepan; stir in tomato sauce. Bring to a boil; reduce heat and simmer 10 minutes. Add meat sauce which has been blended with bouillon. Stir in Worcestershire Sauce and butter; heat. Serve with steaks or chops.

YIELD: APPROXIMATELY 1½ CUPS

MAÎTRE D'HÔTEL BUTTER

Beurre Maître d'Hôtel

¼ CUP SWEET BUTTER
⅛ TEASPOON SALT

1 TEASPOON CHOPPED PARSLEY
1 TABLESPOON LEMON JUICE

⅛ TEASPOON WHITE PEPPER

Cream butter until very soft. Blend in salt, pepper, parsley, and lemon juice. Chill until firm. Use as needed.

YIELD: ¼ CUP

SAUCE VINCENT

Sauce Vincent

4 SPINACH LEAVES
6 SPRIGS WATERCRESS
6 SPRIGS PARSLEY
6 SPRIGS CHERVIL
2 LEAVES TARRAGON

6 CHIVES
3 HARD-COOKED EGG YOLKS
2 UNCOOKED EGG YOLKS
2 TABLESPOONS TARRAGON
  VINEGAR

OLIVE OIL

Blanch spinach, watercress, parsley, chervil, tarragon, and chives in small amount hot, salted water about 5 minutes. Drain; press dry. Pound, or force through a sieve with the hard-cooked egg yolks alternately with the uncooked egg yolks. Gradually stir in tarragon vinegar. Gradually add enough olive oil to make the consistency of mayonnaise. Chill.

YIELD: APPROXIMATELY ½ CUP

BORDELAISE SAUCE

Sauce Bordelaise

2 TABLESPOONS FINELY CHOPPED
  SHALLOTS OR SCALLIONS
1 SMALL CARROT
¾ CUP RED WINE

1 CUP HOT BROWN SAUCE*
1 TABLESPOON BUTTER
1 TABLESPOON LEMON JUICE
1 TABLESPOON FINELY CHOPPED
  PARSLEY

Put shallots, carrots, and wine into a saucepan. Simmer until mixture is reduced to one-half. Strain into hot Brown Sauce. Gradually add butter, bit by bit. Stir in lemon juice and parsley. If desired, poach ¼-inch thick slices beef marrow in beef stock. Place over steak; pour sauce over all.

YIELD: APPROXIMATELY 1½ CUPS

*See page 98

✤ ✤ ✤

MUSTARD BERCY SAUCE

Sauce Bercy à la Moutarde

4 SHALLOTS, FINELY CHOPPED
1 CUP FISH STOCK
1 CUP WHITE WINE

2 TABLESPOONS BUTTER
2 TEASPOONS PREPARED MUSTARD
2 TABLESPOONS FINELY CHOPPED
  PARSLEY

Put shallots into a saucepan; add fish stock and wine. Bring to a boil; boil until liquid is reduced by one-half. Strain into a saucepan. Add butter and mustard; heat, but do not boil. Remove from heat; stir in parsley.

YIELD: APPROXIMATELY 1 CUP

✤ ✤ ✤

MORNAY SAUCE

Sauce Mornay

1 CUP BECHAMEL SAUCE*
¾ CUP WHITE WINE
1 TABLESPOON GRATED PARMESAN
  CHEESE

1 TABLESPOON GRATED SWISS
  CHEESE
1 TABLESPOON BUTTER

Put Bechamel Sauce and wine in saucepan. Reduce to one-third over high heat, constantly stirring. Add cheese. Remove from heat and stir well. Add butter just before using.

YIELD: 2 CUPS

*See page 95

FISH FUMET

Fumet de poisson

¾ POUND FISH HEADS AND
   TRIMMINGS
1 SMALL ONION, THINLY SLICED
5 SPRIGS OF PARSLEY

1 WHOLE CLOVE
1 SMALL BAY LEAF
⅛ TEASPOON PEPPER
2 CUPS WHITE WINE

2 CUPS COLD WATER

Put all ingredients in a saucepan. Bring to a boil and then lower heat. Simmer 30 minutes. Bring to a boil and allow to boil until liquid is reduced to half volume. Strain with fine strainer. Season with salt to taste. Allow to cool before storing if not used immediately.

YIELD: 1 QUART

✤ ✤ ✤

NORMANDY SAUCE

Sauce Normande

1 CUP FISH FUMET*
¼ CUP MUSHROOM STOCK
¼ CUP MUSSEL STOCK
¼ TEASPOON LEMON JUICE

2 EGG YOLKS
5 TABLESPOONS LIGHT CREAM
   DIVIDED
1 TABLESPOON BUTTER

Put Fish Fumet, mushroom and mussel stocks and lemon juice into a saucepan. Boil until mixture is reduced to ¾ cup. Remove from heat. Combine egg yolks with 1 tablespoon of the cream. Add to stock, stirring rapidly. Heat, but do not boil. Strain. Heat remaining cream; add to original mixture with butter.

YIELD: APPROXIMATELY 1 CUP

* See above.

✤ ✤ ✤

SHRIMP BUTTER

Beurre de Crevettes

6 SMALL COOKED SHRIMP

2 TABLESPOONS BUTTER

Place shrimp in small bowl or mortar. Pound until very fine. Add butter and knead until well blended.

YIELD: 4 TABLESPOONS

✤ ✤ ✤

MELTED MUSTARD BUTTER

Beurre Fondu à la Moutarde

½ CUP MELTED, CLARIFIED BUTTER

2 TEASPOONS PREPARED MUSTARD

Gradually blend the butter with mustard. Heat, but do not boil.

YIELD: APPROXIMATELY ½ CUP

Vegetables

Château d'Artigny

❖ ❖ ❖

MUSHROOMS UNDER BELLS   *Champignons sous Cloche*

4 TEASPOONS BUTTER	SHERRY OR MADEIRA WINE
4 SLICES TOAST	2 DOZEN MUSHROOM CAPS

1 CUP HEAVY CREAM, DIVIDED

Place 1 teaspoon butter in the center of each of 4 individual casseroles. Soak toast in sherry or Madeira wine; press dry and place one slice in each casserole. Top each with 6 mushroom caps; sprinkle with salt and freshly ground pepper. Pour ¼ cup cream around the toast in each casserole. Cover. Bake in a 350°F. oven, 30 minutes. At end of 15 minutes, pour in additional cream if necessary.

YIELD: 4 SERVINGS

Note: If toast has not been soaked in wine, add 1 tablespoon wine to each casserole just before serving, if desired.

Hostellerie de la Poste

❖ ❖ ❖

STUFFED MUSHROOMS CARÊME   *Champignons Farcis Carême*

1½ DOZEN LARGE MUSHROOMS	1 CUP BEEF OR CHICKEN GRAVY
4 TABLESPOONS BUTTER	3 EGG YOLKS, SLIGHTLY BEATEN
1 TABLESPOON MINCED SHALLOT	1 TEASPOON EACH MINCED
1 CUP MINCED COOKED LOBSTER	PARSLEY AND CHIVES
1 CUP WHITE WINE	TOAST ROUNDS

ANCHOVY PASTE

Remove stems from mushrooms; coarsely chop. Melt butter in a saucepan; add shallot and lobster. Cook over low heat 5 minutes, stirring occasionally. Add chopped mushroom stems; cook 5 minutes longer. Add wine and cook until mixture is reduced by one-half. Add gravy; boil 8 to 10 minutes. Remove from heat. Add beaten egg yolks, stirring rapidly. Season to taste with salt, pepper and nutmeg. Stir in parsley and chives. Stuff mushroom caps with mixture; place in greased shallow baking pan. Dot with butter. Bake in a 350°F. oven, 10 to 15 minutes. Serve mushrooms on toast rounds which have been spread lightly with anchovy paste.

YIELD: 4 SERVINGS

Château Choiseul

✦ ✦ ✦

MUSHROOMS IN CHICKEN BROTH   *Champignons à la Poulette*

6 TABLESPOONS BUTTER, DIVIDED
2 TABLESPOONS FLOUR
2 CUPS CHICKEN STOCK

3 EGG YOLKS, SLIGHTLY BEATEN
JUICE OF 1 LEMON
1 TEASPOON MINCED PARSLEY

1 POUND MUSHROOMS, SLICED

Melt 2 tablespoons of the butter in a saucepan; blend in flour. Gradually add chicken stock and cook, stirring constantly, until mixture thickens and comes to a boil. Remove from heat; add egg yolks, stirring rapidly. Return to low heat and stir until slightly thickened. Remove from heat; stir in salt and white pepper to taste and lemon juice. Melt remaining 4 tablespoons butter in a saucepan; add mushrooms and cook, stirring occasionally, until tender. Add to sauce; heat to serving temperature. Serve over toast points or in patty shells.

YIELD: 4 SERVINGS

Château Choiseul

✦ ✦ ✦

CREAMED MUSHROOMS WITH HERBS
Champignons Fines Herbes au Gratin

1 POUND MUSHROOMS, SLICED
½ CUP OLIVE OIL
2 TABLESPOONS GRATED ONION
1 TABLESPOON EACH MINCED
  PARSLEY, CHIVES, AND CHERVIL
⅛ TEASPOON EACH DRIED
  TARRAGON, PEPPER, AND THYME

1 GARLIC CLOVE, MASHED
¾ TEASPOON SALT
3 TABLESPOONS TARRAGON
  VINEGAR
⅓ CUP BUTTER
1 CUP BUTTERED BREAD
  CRUMBS

Put all ingredients except butter and bread crumbs into a deep bowl. Let marinate two hours, stirring occasionally. Drain. Melt butter in a skillet. Add mushrooms and cook, stirring occasionally, until tender. Turn into a shallow, buttered baking dish; sprinkle with buttered crumbs. Place under broiler until lightly browned.

YIELD: 4 SERVINGS

Château de Mercuès

✣ ✣ ✣

LYONNAISE MUSHROOMS

Champignons Lyonnaise

1½ POUNDS MUSHROOMS
⅓ CUP BUTTER
1 GARLIC CLOVE
1 BAY LEAF
2 WHOLE CLOVES

1½ CUPS TOMATO SAUCE
½ CUP BEEF STOCK
1 TABLESPOON BUTTER
1 TABLESPOON EACH MINCED
 PARSLEY, CHIVES, AND ONION

Quarter mushrooms. Melt butter in a skillet; add mushrooms, garlic, bay leaf, and whole cloves. Sauté 5 minutes; add tomato sauce, beef stock, salt and pepper to taste. Heat. Turn into a casserole; cover and bake in a 350°F. oven, 25 minutes. Remove garlic, whole cloves, and bay leaf. Cream together butter, parsley, chives, and onion; add bit by bit to casserole. Serve on hot buttered toast; top each serving with a poached egg.

YIELD: 6 SERVINGS

Hostellerie de la Poste

✣ ✣ ✣

FLAMING MUSHROOMS

Champignons Flambés

2 POUNDS MUSHROOM CAPS
¼ POUND BUTTER
⅛ TEASPOON NUTMEG

1 CUP SHERRY WINE
2 WHOLE CLOVES
¼ CUP BRANDY

½ CUP HEAVY CREAM, SCALDED

Cook mushrooms in butter in chafing dish. Sprinkle with salt and pepper to taste and nutmeg. Add sherry and whole cloves; simmer until mushrooms are almost dry. Add brandy; ignite. When flame has gone out, stir in cream. Heat; serve on toast points.

YIELD: 6 TO 8 SERVINGS

Hostellerie du Prieuré

✦ ✦ ✦

ANDALUSIAN MUSHROOMS
Champignons Andalouse

1 POUND MUSHROOMS
⅓ CUP BUTTER
1 POUND DICED COOKED VIRGINIA HAM
⅓ CUP OLIVE OIL
½ CUP SHERRY WINE

2 TABLESPOONS PORT WINE
2 TABLESPOONS DICED PIMENTO
1 TABLESPOON MINCED PARSLEY
1 TABLESPOON BOTTLED THICK MEAT SAUCE
1 TEASPOON LEMON JUICE

Sauté mushrooms in butter until half cooked. Sauté ham in olive oil 5 minutes. Transfer both to a 2½-quart casserole with cover. Pour in wines; sprinkle with pimento and parsley. Bake in a 300°F. oven, 40 minutes, stirring occasionally. Remove from oven; blend in meat sauce and sprinkle with lemon juice.

YIELD: 6 TO 8 SERVINGS

Château de la Fortinière

✦ ✦ ✦

STUFFED MUSHROOM CAPS
Têtes de Champignons Farcies

6 LARGE MUSHROOMS
4 TABLESPOONS BUTTER
  SALT, PEPPER, NUTMEG, SAGE AND THYME
1 EGG, BEATEN

¼ CUP HEAVY CREAM
1 GARLIC CLOVE, MASHED
1½ DOZEN SHELLED, COOKED MUSSELS
1 TABLESPOON MADEIRA WINE

Remove stems from mushrooms. Melt butter in a saucepan; add caps and stems. Sprinkle lightly with salt, pepper, nutmeg, sage, and thyme. Cook until mushrooms are tender, stirring frequently. Remove caps and stems; chop stems very finely. Return stems to saucepan with egg which has been combined with cream and garlic. Cook over low heat, stirring constantly, until thickened. Remove from heat; stir in mussels and wine. Spoon into mushroom caps, using 3 mussels per cap. Sprinkle with buttered bread crumbs; place under broiler until browned.

YIELD: 6 SERVINGS

Château de la Chèvre d'Or

✦ ✦ ✦

NEAPOLITAN STYLE MUSHROOMS   *Champignons Napolitaine*

1 POUND MUSHROOMS
¼ CUP OLIVE OIL

1 GARLIC CLOVE, FINELY CHOPPED
3 TOMATOES, PEELED AND SLICED

Quarter mushrooms. Heat olive oil in a skillet; add mushrooms, garlic, and tomatoes. Cook over medium heat, stirring constantly, about 7 minutes. Season to taste with salt and pepper.

YIELD: 4 SERVINGS

Château de Divonne

✦ ✦ ✦

POTATO SOUFFLÉ   *Pommes Soufflées*

1½ POUNDS POTATOES
1 SMALL CARROT, QUARTERED
1 SMALL PARSNIP, SLICED
1 MEDIUM ONION, SLICED
2 WHOLE CLOVES

1 BOUQUET GARNI
3 TABLESPOONS BUTTER
4 EGGS
2 TABLESPOONS GRATED ONION
   FINELY CHOPPED CHIVES

Put potatoes into a saucepan; add carrot, parsnip, onion, cloves, *bouquet garni*. Add enough water to half cover. Cook over medium heat until potatoes are tender. Drain. Place in a saucepan and dry the potatoes over a low flame to remove all the moisture. Mash with butter, salt and pepper to taste, and enough light cream for mashed-potato consistency. Beat in eggs, one at a time, heating well after each addition; beat in onion. Place over low heat and stir until mixture follows the spoon or forms a ball. Form into balls the size of a walnut, adding to each ball a pinch of chives. Refrigerate overnight. When ready to serve, deep-fry at 375°F., 1 minutes, until balls are puffed and float on the surface of the fat. Drain on absorbent paper. Serve hot as a garnish for fish, meat, poultry, or game or cold as an hors d'oeuvre.

Château de Challes

✤ ✤ ✤

POTATOES DAUPHINOISE

Pommes de Terre Dauphinoise

6 MEDIUM POTATOES   LIGHT CREAM
¼ POUND GRATED SWISS CHEESE

Pare potatoes, trimming them into cylinder shape. Cut crosswise into ⅛-inch thick slices. Butter a large casserole. Layer potatoes into casserole, topping each layer lightly with salt and pepper, sliced garlic clove (2 cloves per layer), and dotting with butter. Pour in enough light cream to fill just to the top, sprinkle with Swiss cheese. Bake in a 450°F. oven, 45 minutes.

YIELD: 6 SERVINGS

Château de Creissels

✤ ✤ ✤

PEAS AND POTATO BALLS

Petits Pois Niçoise

2 CUPS SHELLED PEAS   1 CUP TOMATO JUICE
2 CUPS TINY POTATO BALLS   2 TABLESPOONS BUTTER
1 BOUQUET GARNI   1 TEASPOON FLOUR

Put peas and potato balls into a saucepan. Add *bouquet garni* and tomato juice. Add salt and pepper to taste. Cover; place over low heat and simmer 35 to 40 minutes, stirring occasionally. Blend together butter and flour; add bit by bit to mixture, stirring carefully, until slightly thickened.

YIELD: 6 SERVINGS

Château d'Artigny

❖ ❖ ❖

GOURMET POTATOES

Pommes de Terre Gourmet

3 TABLESPOONS BUTTER
3 EGGS, SEPARATED
3 CUPS HOT, RICED POTATOES

½ CUP GRATED GRUYÈRE CHEESE
1 TEASPOON PREPARED MUSTARD
2 TABLESPOONS FINELY CHOPPED
PARSLEY

Beat butter and egg yolks into hot potatoes; season to taste with salt, pepper, and nutmeg. Add a small amount of light cream if necessary to make a creamy mixture. Spread into a 9-inch pie plate. Beat egg whites until stiff, but not dry; fold in remaining ingredients. Pile on top of potato mixture; sprinkle with paprika. Place under broiler 5 inches from heat until meringue is lightly browned.

YIELD: 6 SERVINGS

Château de la Tortinière

❖ ❖ ❖

SWEET POTATOES IN ORANGE SHELLS

Patate Douce en Coquilles d'Oranges

3 CUPS (4 TO 5) MASHED SWEET
POTATOES
2 EGG YOLKS, SLIGHTLY BEATEN
⅓ CUP ORANGE JUICE

SALT AND PEPPER
¼ TEASPOON NUTMEG
3 TABLESPOONS BUTTER
6 HALF-ORANGE SHELLS

SUGAR

Combine mashed sweet potatoes with egg yolks, orange juice, salt and pepper to taste, and nutmeg and butter. Mix well. Spoon into orange shells. Sprinkle with sugar and dot with butter. Bake in a 350°F. oven, 15 to 20 minutes, or until heated through.

YIELD: 6 SERVINGS

Château d'Ayres

❖ ❖ ❖

SAUSAGE-STUFFED TOMATOES

Tomates Farcies Charcutière

6 LARGE TOMATOES
1 POUND PORK SAUSAGE MEAT
4 CHICKEN LIVERS
1 GARLIC CLOVE, MASHED
1 TABLESPOON EACH MINCED
ONION, CHIVES, AND PARSLEY
½ TEASPOON CHOPPED TARRAGON

1 TEASPOON FINELY CHOPPED
SHALLOT
½ CUP SOFT BREAD CRUMBS
1 EGG, SLIGHTLY BEATEN
1 EGG YOLK, SLIGHTLY BEATEN
⅓ CUP HEAVY CREAM
½ CUP BUTTERED BREAD CRUMBS

Scoop out all the pulp from tomatoes; sprinkle cavities lightly with salt and pepper; reserve. Cook sausage meat in a skillet until browned, breaking up with a fork. Remove cooked sausage; drain fat reserving 2 tablespoons. Add chicken livers and cook until tender, 5 minutes. Remove from skillet; finely chop. Add to sausage with garlic, onion, chives, parsley, tarragon, shallot, and bread crumbs. Add egg, egg yolk, and heavy cream and mix until blended. Divide mixture among tomatoes; sprinkle with buttered bread crumbs. Wrap each tomato in buttered brown paper; twist tops. Place side by side in a shallow baking pan. Add enough red wine to pan to measure an inch and 2 tablespoons butter. Bake in a 375°F. oven, 40 minutes, basting occasionally. Remove paper and bake 15 minutes longer. Transfer to serving platter. Garnish with watercress and pass Brown Sauce.*

YIELD: 6 SERVINGS

*See page 98

Château de Cheronnac

❖ ❖ ❖

TOMATO PIE

Tarte aux Tomates

PASTRY FOR 1-CRUST PIE
6 LARGE, FIRM TOMATOES, SLICED

⅓ TO ½ CUP BUTTER
SALT, PEPPER, CURRY POWDER

Cut a 14-inch circle of aluminum foil; place on baking sheet and flour lightly. Roll out pastry into a 14-inch circle; flute edges if desired. Bake in a 425°F. oven, 10 minutes; remove. Sprinkle tomato slices lightly with salt, pepper, and curry powder. Dredge in flour. Melt butter in a large skillet. Fry quickly on both sides until browned and crisp. Place tomato slices on top of baked pastry, side by side. Bake in a 350°F. oven, 12 to 15 minutes.

YIELD: 6 SERVINGS

Château de Mimont

❖ ❖ ❖

TOMATOES WITH SOUR CREAM

Tomates à la Crème

6 LARGE, FIRM TOMATOES, PEELED
　AND SLICED
SALT
PEPPER
SUGAR

1½ CUPS SOFT BREAD CRUMBS,
　DIVIDED
SLICED ONIONS
1½ CUPS SOUR CREAM
1 TABLESPOON MELTED BUTTER

Place a layer of half the tomato slices in a buttered, shallow baking dish. Sprinkle with salt, pepper, sugar, and ½ cup of the bread crumbs. Add a layer of sliced onions, about ½-inch thick. Repeat with second layer of tomatoes and bread crumbs. Spoon sour cream over top. Combine remaining ½ cup bread crumbs with melted butter; sprinkle over sour cream. Cover. Bake in a 350°F. oven, 45 minutes. Uncover for last 10 to 15 minutes of baking time.

YIELD: 6 SERVINGS

Château d'Artigny

♣ ♣ ♣

CREAMED ONIONS WITH CHESTNUTS

Onions à la Béchamel avec Châtaignes

½ POUND CHESTNUTS
2 POUNDS TINY WHITE ONIONS, PEELED
    CHICKEN STOCK OR WATER
2 CUPS BECHAMEL SAUCE*
3 TABLESPOONS BUTTER
½ CUP BUTTERED BREAD CRUMBS
½ CUP GRATED SWISS CHEESE

Cook chestnuts in water to cover until tender. Shell and place in hot milk for 15 minutes. Drain; coarsely chop nuts. Cook onions in enough chicken stock to cover, 25 to 30 minutes, or until tender; drain. Add to Bechamel Sauce. Sauté nuts in butter; add to onion mixture. Season to taste with salt and pepper. Turn into a buttered 2½-quart casserole; sprinkle with crumbs which have been combined with cheese. Bake in a 400°F. oven, 10 to 15 minutes, or until crumbs are brown and mixture is heated through.

YIELD: 6 SERVINGS

*See page 95

Château de la Chèvre d'Or

♣ ♣ ♣

FRIED STUFFED LETTUCE

Laitues Farcies Frites

12 LARGE LETTUCE LEAVES
½ CUP CHOPPED, COOKED CHICKEN
2 TABLESPOONS GRATED ONION
1 TABLESPOON EACH MINCED PARSLEY AND CHIVES
¼ CUP SOFT BREAD CRUMBS
1 CUP CHOPPED, COOKED MACARONI OR SPAGHETTI
SALT, PEPPER, AND THYME
HEAVY CREAM

Blanch lettuce leaves; drain and reserve. Combine remaining ingredients except salt, pepper, thyme, and cream. Season. Add enough heavy cream to hold together. Divide mixture among the lettuce leaves; roll up and secure with thread every half-inch. Cut into 2-inch pieces, securing the ends. Roll in beaten egg and then in fine dry bread crumbs. Deep-fry at 385°F., 2 minutes, or until lightly browned.

YIELD: 3 TO 4 SERVINGS

L'Oustau de Baumanière

✤ ✤ ✤

SPINACH CROQUETTES

Croquettes d'Épinards

2 CUPS COOKED SPINACH
3 TABLESPOONS BUTTER
1 TABLESPOON FLOUR
¾ CUP LIGHT CREAM, DIVIDED

4 EGG YOLKS, DIVIDED
SALT, PEPPER, AND NUTMEG
¼ CUP GROUND ALMONDS
2 TABLESPOONS RICED POTATOES

½ TEASPOON SHERRY WINE

Chop spinach very fine. Melt butter in saucepan; blend in flour. Beat together ¼ cup of the cream and 2 egg yolks. Blend into flour mixture; add chopped spinach. Cook, stirring constantly, until mixture thickens. Season to taste with salt, pepper, and nutmeg. Spread on a platter; chill. Put remaining ½ cup cream and almonds in a saucepan; bring to a boil. Reduce heat and simmer 3 minutes, stirring occasionally. Strain through several thicknesses of cheesecloth. Return the almond milk to the saucepan. Add potatoes and cook, stirring constantly, until mixture is smooth and thick. Remove from heat; beat in remaining 2 egg yolks, sherry, and salt and pepper to taste. Cool. Form spinach into small oblong croquettes; wrap potato mixture around each croquette. Dip croquettes in beaten egg, then in crumbs; repeat. Deep-fry at 380°F. until delicately browned.

YIELD: 4 SERVINGS

Hostellerie de la Poste

✤ ✤ ✤

SPINACH CONTI

Epinards Conti

2 POUNDS SPINACH
6 EGGS, WELL BEATEN
SALT, PEPPER, AND NUTMEG

Wash spinach thoroughly; place in a saucepan without adding water. Cover; cook over low heat, 10 minutes, stirring once. Remove from heat; drain. Season to taste with salt, pepper, and nutmeg. Return to saucepan and cook over very low heat to evaporate excess moisture. Add eggs and cook over medium heat, stirring constantly, until of scrambled-egg consistency.

YIELD: 6 TO 8 SERVINGS

Hostellerie de la Poste

⚜ ⚜ ⚜

SPINACH SOUFFLÉ WITH ALMONDS *Soufflé d'Epinards aux Amandes*

3 TABLESPOONS BUTTER
4 TABLESPOONS FLOUR
½ TEASPOON SALT
¼ TEASPOON PEPPER
  DASH MACE

1 CUP ALMOND MILK*
½ TEASPOON WORCESTERSHIRE
  SAUCE
2 CUPS FINELY CHOPPED COOKED
  SPINACH

3 EGGS, SEPARATED

Melt butter in a saucepan; blend in flour, salt, pepper, and mace. Gradually add almond milk and Worcestershire Sauce and cook, stirring occasionally, until mixture thickens and comes to a boil. Remove from heat. Stir in spinach; blend well. Beat in egg yolks, one at a time. Beat egg whites until stiff, but not dry; fold into spinach mixture. Turn into a soufflé dish. Bake in a 350°F. oven, 35 to 40 minutes. Serve immediately.

YIELD: 4 SERVINGS

*To make almond milk, grind ¼ cup blanched almonds and place in saucepan. Add 1 cup milk and bring to a boil. Reduce heat to very low and simmer 15 minutes. Strain.

Le Prieuré

⚜ ⚜ ⚜

ENDIVES MORNAY

Endives Mornay

2 POUNDS ENDIVE
  JUICE OF 1 LEMON
1½ TEASPOONS SALT

4 TABLESPOONS BUTTER, DIVIDED
1 CUP WATER
2 CUPS MORNAY SAUCE*

Place endives in a deep saucepan. Add lemon juice, salt, 3 tablespoons of the butter, and water. Cover; cook 35 minutes or until tender. Drain. Place in buttered shallow baking pan; top with Mornay Sauce. Dot with remaining butter. Place under broiler until lightly browned.

YIELD: 4 TO 6 SERVINGS

*See page 101

Château de Coudrée

✦ ✦ ✦

EGGPLANT PARIS STYLE

Aubergine Parisienne

3 SMALL EGGPLANT
   DICED COOKED CHICKEN, VEAL,
   OR PORK
¾ CUP SOFT BREAD CRUMBS

2 TABLESPOONS DICED GREEN
   PEPPER
¼ CUP GROUND SUET
3 EGG YOLKS
   BUTTERED BREAD CRUMBS

Halve eggplant lengthwise; scoop out pulp. Rub inside surface of shells with a cut clove of garlic; sprinkle lightly with salt, pepper, nutmeg, and powdered thyme. Force enough chicken, or equal parts of chicken, veal, and pork, through a food chopper, using finest blade, to make 2 cups. Repeat with bread crumbs, eggplant pulp, and green pepper. Combine ground ingredients in a bowl; add suet and stir in egg yolks. Season with salt, pepper, and nutmeg. Pile into eggplant shells; sprinkle with buttered crumbs. Bake in a 350°F. oven, 35 to 40 minutes, or until heated through.

YIELD: 6 SERVINGS

Château de Pray

✦ ✦ ✦

EGGPLANT CASSEROLE

Aubergines en Casserole

1 MEDIUM EGGPLANT
½ CUP OLIVE OIL, DIVIDED
12 ANCHOVY FILLETS
2 MEDIUM ONIONS, SLICED
6 SLICES HAM
1 LARGE GREEN PEPPER, SLICED

2 GARLIC CLOVES, FINELY
   CHOPPED
1 CAN (20 OUNCES) TOMATOES
2 BAY LEAVES
2 WHOLE CLOVES
½ CUP GRATED CHEESE
   ½ CUP BUTTERED FINE BREAD CRUMBS

Cut eggplant crosswise into 6 slices; pare if desired. Heat ¼ cup of the olive oil in a skillet; add eggplant slices and brown on both sides. Place 3 of the slices in bottom of a large, greased casserole. Top with half the anchovies, onion, ham, and pepper slices. Sprinkle with half the garlic. Repeat. Pour tomatoes into casserole. Add bay leaf, cloves, and remaining ¼ cup olive oil. Cover; bake in a 350°F. oven, 40 to 45 minutes. Uncover. Combine cheese and bread crumbs; sprinkle over top. Place under broiler until browned.

YIELD: 4 TO 6 SERVINGS

La Petite Auberge

✦ ✦ ✦

RATATOUILLE

Ratatouille Avignonaise

OLIVE OIL

2 POUNDS EGGPLANTS,
PEELED AND SLICED

1 POUND SQUASH,
PEELED AND SLICED

1 POUND GREEN PEPPER, SLICED

2 POUNDS TOMATOES,
QUARTERED BUT NOT PEELED

4 OR 5 GARLIC CLOVES, CRUSHED

2 ONIONS, SLICED

1 LARGE BOUQUET GARNI
(PARSLEY, THYME, TARRAGON,
CELERY, BAY LEAF)

1 TEASPOON TARRAGON,
CHOPPED

SALT AND PEPPER

Sauté lightly in olive oil the eggplant, squash, and green pepper in deep saucepan. Add tomatoes, garlic, *bouquet garni,* and tarragon. Cover. Simmer over low heat for one hour. Serve hot. In summer it may be served cold.

YIELD: 12 SERVINGS

Château de Pray

✦ ✦ ✦

MIXED BEANS BRITTANY

Haricots Panachés Bretonne

½ CUP DRIED LIMA BEANS

½ CUP DRIED NAVY BEANS

½ CUP DRIED KIDNEY BEANS

½ CUP BLACK BEANS

½ POUND FRESH GREEN BEANS,
CUT JULIENNE STYLE

½ CUP FRESH LIMA BEANS

⅓ CUP BUTTER

2 TABLESPOONS LEMON JUICE

2 TABLESPOONS EACH FINELY
CHOPPED PARSLEY AND CHIVES

Soak dried beans overnight; drain. Cook all vegetables separately in water seasoned with salt, pepper, sliced onion, pinch of dill, and piece of bay leaf, until tender. Drain; reserve liquid as a base for soup. Melt butter in a large skillet; add beans and cook until heated through, stirring occasionally. When ready to serve, stir in lemon juice, parsley, and chives.

YIELD: 8 TO 10 SERVINGS

Château de la Vallée Bleue

✦ ✦ ✦

CUCUMBER RING MOLDS *Couronnes de Concombres en Gelée Paris-Plage*

4 LARGE CUCUMBERS
2 CUPS CHICKEN STOCK, DIVIDED
1 WHOLE CLOVE
1 GARLIC CLOVE, MASHED
1 TABLESPOON ONION JUICE
1 BAY LEAF

6 SPRIGS PARSLEY
1 ENVELOPE UNFLAVORED GELATIN
1 TABLESPOON TARRAGON VINEGAR
1 CUP MAYONNAISE
1 TABLESPOON CAVIAR
1 TABLESPOON TOMATO PASTE

2 TABLESPOONS CAPERS

Pare and slice cucumbers; place in a deep saucepan. Add 1½ cups of the chicken stock, whole clove, garlic, onion juice, bay leaf, and parsley. Season to taste with salt and pepper. Bring to a boil; reduce heat and simmer until tender. Force through a sieve into a mixing bowl. Sprinkle gelatin on remaining ½ cup of chicken stock to soften. Add to hot mixture and stir until gelatin is dissolved. Stir in vinegar. Pour into 6 individual ring molds; chill until firm. When ready to serve, unmold on chilled serving platter. Combine mayonnaise with remaining ingredients; spoon into center of rings. Garnish with watercress.

YIELD: 6 SERVINGS

Château St. Jean

✦ ✦ ✦

BRUSSELS SPROUTS LYONNAISE *Choux de Bruxelles Lyonnaise*

3 TABLESPOONS BUTTER
1 MEDIUM ONION, SLICED
⅓ CUP CHICKEN STOCK

1 QUART COOKED BRUSSELS
SPROUTS
1 TABLESPOON EACH MINCED
PARSLEY AND CHIVES

Melt butter in a large skillet. Add onion and cook until tender, but not brown. Add chicken stock and brussels sprouts. Season with salt, white pepper, and a dash of cayenne. Heat, stirring constantly, until liquid is absorbed. Turn into serving dish; sprinkle with parsley and chives.

YIELD: 6 TO 8 SERVINGS

Vegetables • 119

Desserts

Château d'Ayres

✤ ✤ ✤

CRÈME AU KIRSCH

Crème au Kirsch

1 CUP SUGAR
8 EGG YOLKS
1 CUP SHERRY WINE
½ CUP WATER

¼ CUP KIRSCH
1 TEASPOON GRATED LEMON RIND
½ CUP HEAVY CREAM
½ CUP MILK

½ CUP CHOPPED UNSALTED NUTS

Beat together sugar and egg yolks until thick and lemon colored. Gradually beat in wine, water, kirsch, and lemon rind. When blended, beat in cream and milk. Turn into top of a double boiler over hot, not boiling water. Cook, stirring constantly, until mixture coats spoon. Remove from water; cool slightly and stir in nuts. Pour into serving dish; chill thoroughly.

YIELD: 8 SERVINGS

Château de Challes

✤ ✤ ✤

CHOCOLATE CREAM

Crème Chocolat

1 ENVELOPE UNFLAVORED GELATIN
½ CUP SUGAR
⅛ TEASPOON SALT
1½ CUPS MILK

1 SQUARE UNSWEETENED
  CHOCOLATE, GRATED
½ TEASPOON VANILLA
1 CUP HEAVY CREAM, WHIPPED

Mix together gelatin, sugar, and salt in a saucepan; stir in milk; add grated chocolate. Cook over low heat, stirring constantly, until gelatin and sugar are thoroughly dissolved and chocolate is melted. Remove from heat. Add vanilla and beat with a rotary beater until flecks of chocolate disappear. Chill until mixture begins to mound. Fold in whipped cream. Turn into a 3-cup mold; chill until firm. Unmold and garnish with additional whipped cream.

YIELD: 6 SERVINGS

Château de Coudrée

✦ ✦ ✦

FRENCH COFFEE BAVARIAN CREAM
Bavarois au Café

1 ENVELOPE UNFLAVORED GELATIN
2 TABLESPOONS INSTANT COFFEE
6 TABLESPOONS SUGAR, DIVIDED
1¼ CUPS MILK, DIVIDED
2 EGGS, SEPARATED
1 TABLESPOON RUM
1 CUP HEAVY CREAM, WHIPPED

Mix together gelatin, coffee, and 2 tablespoons of the sugar in top of double boiler. Beat together milk and egg yolks; add to double boiler. Place over boiling water and cook, stirring constantly, until gelatin is dissolved and mixture thickens slightly. Remove from water; stir in rum. Chill until mixture begins to mound. Beat egg whites until stiff, but not dry. Gradually add remaining 4 tablespoons sugar and beat until very stiff. Fold into gelatin mixture; fold in whipped cream. Turn into a 6-cup mold; chill until firm. When ready to serve, unmold on a chilled serving platter. Garnish with additional whipped cream and if desired, sprinkle cream lightly with instant coffee.

YIELD: 8 SERVINGS

Château de Divonne

✦ ✦ ✦

COFFEE CREAM COUPE
Coupe de Crème au Café

2 CUPS WATER
½ CUP GROUND COFFEE
⅛ TEASPOON SALT
½ CUP SUGAR
½ TEASPOON VANILLA
2 CUPS HEAVY CREAM, WHIPPED
CHOPPED PISTACHIO NUTS

Bring water to a boil in a saucepan. Gradually add coffee, salt, and sugar. Remove from heat; stir until sugar is dissolved. Let stand 30 minutes. Strain through several thicknesses of cheesecloth; stir in vanilla. Chill. Fold in whipped cream. Turn into refrigerator trays. Freeze until almost firm. Spoon into champagne coupes or sherbet glasses. Top with additional whipped cream and sprinkle with chopped pistachio nuts.

YIELD: APPROXIMATELY 1½ QUARTS

Château de Mimont

✤ ✤ ✤

TEA RUM MOLD

Crème de Thé au Rhum

2 ENVELOPES UNFLAVORED
   GELATIN
1 TABLESPOON INSTANT TEA
⅛ TEASPOON SALT

½ CUP SUGAR
2½ CUPS MILK, DIVIDED
⅓ CUP RUM
1 CUP HEAVY CREAM

Mix together gelatin, tea, salt, and sugar in a saucepan. Stir in 1½ cups of the milk. Place over low heat, stirring constantly, until gelatin and sugar are dissolved. Remove from heat; stir in remaining milk and rum. Chill until mixture begins to mound. Whip cream; fold into gelatin mixture. Turn into 6 individual molds or into serving dish; chill until firm. Unmold if molded; garnish with additional whipped cream.

YIELD: 4 TO 6 SERVINGS

Château de Betz

✤ ✤ ✤

CARAMEL CREAM WITH CRUSHED STRAWBERRIES

Crème Brulée à la Purée de Fraises

2 TEASPOONS FLOUR
¼ CUP SUGAR
¼ TEASPOON SALT
1 CUP MILK
1 CUP HEAVY CREAM

¾ TEASPOON VANILLA
6 EGG YOLKS
   CINNAMON
6 TEASPOONS SUGAR, DIVIDED
   CRUSHED STRAWBERRIES SOAKED
   IN KIRSCH

Mix together flour, sugar, and salt in top of double boiler. Stir in milk and cream. Place over hot water, stirring occasionally, until heated through. Remove from water; stir in vanilla. Add egg yolks, one at a time, beating rapidly. Place over hot water and cook, stirring constantly, until mixture thickens. Turn into 6 buttered individual custard cups. Sprinkle lightly with cinnamon; sprinkle each with 1 teaspoon sugar. Place on baking sheets and bake in a 450°F. oven, 8 to 10 minutes, or until top is well browned and caramelized. Cool. Unmold on serving platter and surround with crushed strawberries which have been flavored with kirsch and sweetened to taste.

YIELD: 6 SERVINGS

Le Prieuré

❖ ❖ ❖

PRIMEROSE CREAM

Crème Primevère

1 ENVELOPE UNFLAVORED GELATIN	½ CUP STRAINED STRAWBERRY JUICE
⅓ CUP SUGAR	½ TEASPOON GRATED LEMON RIND
2½ CUPS MILK	
3 EGG YOLKS, BEATEN	¼ CUP BRANDY

Mix together gelatin and sugar in top of double boiler. Stir in remaining ingredients. Place over boiling water and cook, stirring constantly, until gelatin dissolves and mixture is thickened. Pour into a 4-cup mold; chill until firm. Unmold and garnish with strawberries and whipped cream.

YIELD: 6 TO 8 SERVINGS

Château d'Artigny

❖ ❖ ❖

CHESTNUT CREAM

Crème aux Marrons

1 POUND CHESTNUTS, SHELLED PARBOILED, AND SKINNED	1 TEASPOON VANILLA
	1 ENVELOPE UNFLAVORED GELATIN
3 CUPS MILK, DIVIDED	½ CUP SUGAR
1 TEASPOON LEMON RIND	4 EGG YOLKS
¼ TEASPOON SALT	¼ CUP MARASCHINO LIQUEUR

1 CUP HEAVY CREAM, WHIPPED

Put chestnuts and 2 cups of the milk in a deep saucepan, with lemon rind, salt, and vanilla. Place over low heat and cook, stirring occasionally, until chestnuts are tender. While chestnuts are cooking, mix together gelatin and sugar in a saucepan. Stir in remaining 1 cup milk. Place over low heat and cook, stirring occasionally, until gelatin and sugar are dissolved. Remove from heat; cool slightly. Add egg yolks, one at a time, beating constantly. Return to low heat and cook, stirring constantly, until mixture thickens. Cool. Drain chestnuts and force through a sieve. Add to gelatin mixture with maraschino liqueur. Add a few drops red food coloring to tint pink. Fold in whipped cream. Turn into a large mold which has been decorated with small pieces of fancifully cut angelica, maraschino cherries, candied pineapple, citron, etc., cut with small French vegetable cutters. Chill until firm. Unmold on chilled serving platter and spoon whipped cream around base of mold.

YIELD: 6 TO 8 SERVINGS

L'Oustau de Baumanière

✦ ✦ ✦

CRÈME FRITE CHAMBERLAIN FLAMBÉE

Crème Frite Chamberlain Flambée

2 CUPS SIFTED ALL-PURPOSE
  FLOUR
½ TEASPOON SALT
  DASH CINNAMON, NUTMEG, AND
  GINGER
6 EGGS, DIVIDED
1 CUP MILK

1 TEASPOON GRATED LEMON RIND
2 TABLESPOONS MELTED BUTTER
1 TEASPOON ORANGE FLOWER
  WATER
4 EGG YOLKS
½ CUP CRUMBLED MACAROONS
½ CUP BENEDICTINE

½ CUP BRANDY

Sift flour, salt, and spices into a mixing bowl. Make a well in the center
and add 2 of the eggs; mix thoroughly. Beat remaining whole eggs with
milk, lemon rind, and butter; gradually add to flour mixture, beating until
blended. Turn into a saucepan and cook over very low heat, just until
mixture begins to thicken. Remove immediately; cool to lukewarm.
Stir in flower water; and beat in egg yolks, one at a time, alternately with
macaroon crumbs. Spread about ⅛-inch thick on a platter and chill until
firm. When firm cut into desired shapes with a 2-inch cutter. Dip pieces
into beaten egg yolks diluted with a little milk flavored with curaçao.
Deep-fry at 390°F., 1 minute. Drain on absorbent paper and place on a
napkin on serving platter. Put Benedictine and brandy in top of chafing
dish. Thread some of the fritters on a fork. Ignite Benedictine-brandy
mixture and place the fritters in the mixture. Repeat. Dip in melted
butter; serve immediately.

Château de Mercuès

✦ ✦ ✦

STRAWBERRY CUSTARD WITH KIRSCH *Fraises à la Crème au Kirsch*

1 DOZEN MACAROONS
  KIRSCH

1 PINT STRAWBERRIES
2 CUPS SOFT CUSTARD

Soak macaroons in kirsch. Place in a 1½-quart casserole. Wash and
hull strawberries; place over macaroons. Top with custard. Chill.

YIELD: 4 TO 6 SERVINGS

Château de la Vallée Bleue

✦ ✦ ✦

CREAM CHARLOTTE DUCHESSE

Charlotte Duchesse

6 EGG YOLKS
¼ CUP SUGAR
⅛ TEASPOON SALT

¼ CUP SHERRY WINE
½ TEASPOON VANILLA
2 CUPS HEAVY CREAM, WHIPPED

Place egg yolks in top of double boiler. Add sugar and salt and beat until very thick. Gradually beat in sherry. Place over hot water and beat just until mixture begins to thicken. Remove from heat; stir in vanilla and cool. Turn into refrigerator trays; freeze until almost firm. Turn into a chilled bowl; fold in heavy cream. Spoon into champagne coupes or sherbet glasses which have been lined with split lady fingers dipped quickly into maraschino cherry syrup. Top with additional whipped cream.

YIELD: APPROXIMATELY 2 QUARTS.

Château de Trigance

✦ ✦ ✦

CARAMEL BISQUE

Bisque Caramel

⅔ CUP WATER, DIVIDED
1 CUP SUGAR, DIVIDED
2½ CUPS EVAPORATED MILK,
    DIVIDED

2 EGGS, SLIGHTLY BEATEN
¼ TEASPOON SALT
2 TABLESPOONS VANILLA
½ CUP CHOPPED PISTACHIO NUTS

Put ⅓ cup of the water and ⅔ cup of the sugar in a skillet. Cook until sugar dissolves and boil until mixture becomes caramelized. Heat remaining ⅓ cup water, remaining ⅓ cup sugar, and 1 cup of the evaporated milk in top of double boiler; blend in caramelized mixture. Pour in a stream over beaten eggs, stirring constantly. Return to double boiler and cook until mixture thickens slightly and coats the spoon. Strain and cool. Stir in remaining 1½ cups evaporated milk, salt, vanilla, and pistachio nuts. Turn into freezer trays; freeze until firm.

YIELD: APPROXIMATELY 1 QUART

Château de Mercuès

✦ ✦ ✦

CHERRY PUDDING
Pouding aux Cerises

1 CAN (1 POUND) SOUR, PITTED CHERRIES	2 TABLESPOONS COLD WATER
1¼ CUPS SUGAR	⅛ TEASPOON SALT
1 TEASPOON UNFLAVORED GELATIN	¼ TEASPOON ALMOND EXTRACT
	2 EGG WHITES, UNBEATEN AND CHILLED

1½ CUPS HEAVY CREAM, WHIPPED

Put cherries and sugar into a saucepan. Cook, stirring constantly, until sugar is dissolved. Sprinkle gelatin on water to soften; add to hot cherry mixture and stir until gelatin is dissolved. Stir in salt and almond extract. Chill until cooled, but not stiff. Add unbeaten egg whites and beat with a rotary beater, until mixture begins to stiffen. Fold in whipped cream. Turn into freezer trays; freeze until firm.

YIELD: APPROXIMATELY 1½ QUARTS

Château de Cheronnac

✦ ✦ ✦

CHERRY PUDDING LIMOUSIN
Clafoutis du Limousin aux Cerises

⅔ CUP ALL-PURPOSE FLOUR	3 EGGS, BEATEN
⅔ CUP FINE GRANULATED SUGAR	3 CUPS MILK
¼ TEASPOON SALT	1 POUND PITTED BLACK CHERRIES

Sift flour, sugar, and salt into a mixing bowl. Make a well in the middle and add eggs and milk. Mix with a wooden spoon, taking in a little of the flour mixture at a time to prevent lumping. Mixture should be smooth. Fold in the cherries. Butter a large casserole; turn in the cherry mixture. Spread evenly. Bake in a 400°F. oven, 30 minutes, or until top begins to turn a delicate brown. Remove from oven; sprinkle top with confectioners' sugar.

YIELD: 6 SERVINGS

Château Choiseul

✦ ✦ ✦

STRAWBERRY SHERBET WITH SAUTERNE

Sorbet de Fraises au Sauterne

1 QUART STRAWBERRIES
1 CUP SUGAR
1 CUP SAUTERNE WINE

¼ TEASPOON SALT
JUICE OF 1 ORANGE
JUICE OF 1 LEMON

Wash and hull strawberries. Crush the strawberries while adding sugar. Let stand ½ hour. Drain the pulp into a saucepan; add sauterne. Bring just to a boil; remove from heat. Strain through a fine sieve, pressing well to extract all the juice and part of the pulp, but no seeds. Chill. Stir in salt and orange and lemon juice. Freeze in a crank freezer using 5 parts ice to 3 parts rock salt, until difficult to turn. Spoon into a large chilled pineapple which has been hollowed out. Garnish with additional strawberries.

YIELD: 4 TO 6 SERVINGS

Château de Coudrée

✦ ✦ ✦

BAR-LE-DUC SHERBET

Sorbet Bar le Duc

1 PINT CURRANTS
1 PINT RASPBERRIES
1 CUP WHITE WINE
1½ CUPS SUGAR

2 TABLESPOONS LEMON JUICE
2 TABLESPOONS CHARTREUSE
½ TEASPOON EACH GRATED
    ORANGE AND LEMON RIND

2 EGG WHITES

Wash and stem currants and raspberries. Place in a saucepan; add wine. Bring to a boil; reduce heat and simmer 5 minutes. Strain. Add remaining ingredients except egg whites; let stand 30 minutes. Crush mixture; mix well. Turn into refrigerator trays. Freeze until mixture forms ice crystals on bottom and sides. Beat egg whites with a dash of salt until stiff but not dry. Beat fruit mixture in a chilled bowl until smooth, but not melted. Fold in egg whites. Return to trays and freeze until firm. Serve garnished with minced candied fruit.

YIELD: APPROXIMATELY 1 QUART

Château de Creissels

✤ ✤ ✤

LOVE PARFAIT

Parfait d'Amour

2 CUPS WATER
1 CUP SUGAR
1 CUP ORANGE JUICE
2 TABLESPOONS LEMON JUICE
1 TABLESPOON GRATED ORANGE
   RIND

GRENADINE
CHERRY CORDIAL
BRANDY
WHIPPED CREAM

Put water and sugar in a saucepan. Cook over low heat, stirring constantly, until sugar is dissolved. Remove from heat; stir in orange juice, lemon juice, and rind. Cool; strain. Pour into refrigerator trays; freeze until mixture forms ice crystals on bottom and sides. Beat in a chilled bowl until smooth, but not melted. Return to trays and freeze until firm. When ready to serve, spoon into chilled parfait glasses; with back of spoon make an indentation in top of each. Into each, spoon in order given 1 teaspoon grenadine, then 1 teaspoon cherry cordial, and ½ teaspoon brandy. Force whipped cream through pastry tube around edge of each parfait.

YIELD: 6 TO 8 PARFAITS

Château de Pilate et Fontager

✤ ✤ ✤

CHOCOLATE BISCUIT GLACÉ

Biscuit Glacé au Chocolat

⅓ CUP SUGAR
2 TABLESPOONS HEAVY CREAM
1 TABLESPOON MILK
⅛ TEASPOON SALT

2 SQUARES UNSWEETENED
   CHOCOLATE, GRATED
6 EGG YOLKS, WELL BEATEN
1 TEASPOON VANILLA

2 CUPS HEAVY CREAM, WHIPPED

Mix together sugar, 2 tablespoons heavy cream, milk, salt, and chocolate in top of double boiler. Place over boiling water, stirring constantly, until sugar and chocolate are dissolved. Beat with rotary beater until blended. While beating, gradually beat in beaten egg yolks. Cool. When cold, fold in whipped cream. Turn into a 9-inch square pan; freeze until firm.

YIELD: APPROXIMATELY 1½ QUARTS

Château de la Tortinière

✦ ✦ ✦

ICED ORANGE SNOW BALLS

Oranges Glacées Boules de Neige

6 SMALL ORANGES
1 CUP MINTED FONDANT STICKS
1 CUP TOASTED SLIVERED ALMONDS
4 EGG WHITES

¼ TEASPOON SALT
1 CUP SUGAR, DIVIDED
1 TABLESPOON COINTREAU
LIQUEUR

Select oranges of the same size as possible. Carefully remove rind and skin. Have fondant sticks the same size as almond slivers. Force alternately into the oranges; pressing well so they don't show. Beat egg whites and salt until stiff, but not dry. Gradually add ¾ cup of the sugar and beat until very stiff. Turn meringue into top of double boiler over hot, not boiling, water. Fold in remaining ¼ cup sugar; beat in Cointreau. Pass a thread in the center of each orange. Dip each into the meringue mixture, coating about ½-inch thick, then carefully tie the ends of thread to a long, slender wooden stick. Place in front of the open broiling oven, open hot oven, or in front of flame in the fireplace. The oranges should hang until the meringue is glazed all over, about 45 minutes. Do not have the heat too strong, lest the meringue gets a too deep brown. To eat, place each orange on a plate with a fork stuck into it, and bite into the orange Spanish fashion.

YIELD: 6 SERVINGS

Hostellerie de la Poste

✦ ✦ ✦

GOURMET STRAWBERRIES

Fraises des Gourmets

1 QUART STRAWBERRIES
½ CUP ANISETTE LIQUEUR
½ CUP SUGAR

½ CUP FLOUR
2 CUPS MILK
3 EGGS, SLIGHTLY BEATEN

2 CUPS HEAVY CREAM, WHIPPED

Wash and hull strawberries; put into a bowl. Pour anisette over strawberries. Refrigerate 2 hours, stirring occasionally. Mix together sugar and flour in top of double boiler. Gradually stir in milk; add eggs. Cook over hot water, stirring constantly, until mixture thickens. Remove from heat; cool. Fold in whipped cream; fold in strawberries with liquid; turn into serving bowl; chill. When ready to serve, garnish with additional whipped cream and several whole strawberries.

YIELD: 8 TO 10 SERVINGS

Château de la Chèvre d'Or

✦ ✦ ✦

STRAWBERRIES BENEDICTINE
Fraises des Bénédictins

2 PINTS STRAWBERRIES
2 CUPS MILK
  DASH SALT
¼ CUP HEAVY CREAM
¼ CUP SUGAR
¼ CUP BENEDICTINE
6 EGG YOLKS

Wash and hull strawberries; place in a 2-quart casserole. Chill. Put milk, salt, and sugar in top of double boiler. Heat milk just until scalded; stir in Benedictine. Beat together egg yolks and cream. Very gradually add to milk mixture, stirring briskly, until thickened. Remove from water and stir constantly, until mixture begins to cool. Pour over strawberries; chill.

YIELD: 8 TO 10 SERVINGS

Hostellerie du Prieuré

✦ ✦ ✦

ICED PEACHES ALEXANDRA
Pêches Glacées Alexandra

1 PINT STRAWBERRIES
½ CUP CURRANT JELLY
1 TABLESPOON BRANDY
10 FRESH PEACHES
1¼ CUPS SUGAR, DIVIDED
4 EGG WHITES
¼ TEASPOON SALT
1 TABLESPOON MARASCHINO LIQUEUR OR 2 TEASPOONS FORBIDDEN FRUIT
POUND CAKE SLICES

Wash and hull strawberries; drain and mash. Force through a sieve with currant jelly; stir in brandy. Place in shallow oblong pan; put in freezer. Peel peaches; form into balls with a French ball cutter. Roll peach balls in ½ cup of the sugar. Place symmetrically on top of strawberry mixture and push halfway through. Freeze. Beat egg whites with salt until stiff but not dry. Gradually add remaining ¾ cup sugar, 2 tablespoons at a time, and beat until very stiff. Just before adding last 2 tablespoons sugar, beat in maraschino liqueur. Form into small meringues by forcing through a pastry bag into some hot milk in a shallow pan. Bake in a 325°F. oven, until delicately browned. Remove with slotted spatula and set aside to cool. When ready to serve cut pound cake slices into circles with a biscuit cutter; place on an individual dessert plate. Cut frozen mixture with the same cutter and place on top of cake. Surround each serving with 3 small meringues. Serve with crushed strawberries.

YIELD: 6 SERVINGS

Desserts • 133

Château St. Jean

✤ ✤ ✤

PANCAKE SOUFFLÉ WITH RASPBERRIES OR STRAWBERRIES
Pannequets Soufflés aux Framboises ou aux Fraises

| RASPBERRIES OR STRAWBERRIES | BRANDY |
| 2 EGG WHITES | CONFECTIONERS SUGAR |

Wash fruit; hull strawberries. Soak a few minutes in brandy. Drain and roll in sugar; reserve. Prepare batter for Pannequets Frits.* Beat egg whites until stiff with a dash of salt and fold into batter. Drop one tablespoon of the batter into a hot buttered small skillet. As soon as bottom begins to get firm remove from skillet and place 5 or 6 of the berries on top and pour over another tablespoon batter. Place under the broiler or in a very hot oven until top is firm and delicately brown. Brush with melted butter and sprinkle with granulated sugar. Return to broiler or oven until sugar begins to caramelize. Repeat.

YIELD: 4 SERVINGS

*See page 141

Le Prieuré

✤ ✤ ✤

BRANDY CHEESE SOUFFLÉ FLAMBÉ   *Soufflé au Fromage Flambé*

| 1 CUP BECHAMEL SAUCE* | 3 EGGS, SEPARATED |
| ½ CUP GRATED SWISS OR PARMESAN CHEESE | 5 TABLESPOONS BRANDY, DIVIDED |

Prepare Bechamel Sauce. While still hot, stir in cheese and 3 well-beaten egg yolks and 3 tablespoons of the brandy. Beat egg whites until stiff but not dry with a dash of cinnamon and cayenne; fold into yolk mixture and turn into a buttered soufflé dish. Bake in a 400°F. oven, 30 minutes. When ready to serve, pour remaining 2 tablespoons brandy into a ladle. Ignite and flame over the soufflé.

YIELD: 2 SERVINGS

*See page 95

Château de Creissels

❖ ❖ ❖

LEMON SOUFFLÉ

Soufflé au Citron

3 TABLESPOONS BUTTER
5 TABLESPOONS FLOUR
¼ TEASPOON SALT

1 CUP MILK
RIND AND JUICE OF 1 LEMON
3 EGGS, SEPARATED

6 TABLESPOONS SUGAR

Melt butter in top of double boiler over direct heat; blend in flour and salt. Add milk and cook, stirring constantly. When mixture begins to thicken, place over boiling water and cook until very thick. Remove from heat. Cool slightly and stir in grated lemon rind and juice. Beat egg yolks until light with the sugar; stir into the lemon mixture. Beat egg whites until stiff, but not dry; fold in. Turn into a buttered soufflé dish. Bake in a 350°F. oven until center, when tested with a knife, is firm. Serve with Lemon Sauce or whipped cream.

YIELD: 4 TO 6 SERVINGS

❖ ❖ ❖

LEMON SAUCE

Sauce au Citron

1 CUP WATER
1 TEASPOON GRATED LEMON RIND
⅓ CUP LEMON JUICE

⅔ CUP SUGAR
⅛ TEASPOON SALT
4 EGG YOLKS, SLIGHTLY BEATEN

Put water, lemon rind, lemon juice, sugar, and salt in top of double boiler. Place over direct heat, stirring constantly, until sugar is dissolved. Remove from heat; add small amount of the hot mixture to egg yolks, stirring rapidly. Return to double boiler and cook over hot water, stirring constantly, until mixture coats a spoon. Cool.

YIELD: APPROXIMATELY 2 CUPS

Château d'Artigny

✤ ✤ ✤

GLAZED CHERRY PIE
Tartelettes aux Cerises Glacées

1 POUND CHERRIES	1 TEASPOON LEMON JUICE
¼ CUP SUGAR	¼ TEASPOON LEMON RIND
¼ CUP WHITE WINE	2 TABLESPOONS FLOUR
½ CUP WATER, DIVIDED	8 BAKED TART SHELLS

Stem and pit cherries. Place in a saucepan with sugar, wine, ¼ cup of the water, lemon juice, and rind. Bring to a boil; boil 5 minutes, stirring constantly. Remove from heat. Blend together flour and remaining ¼ cup of water. Stir into cherry mixture. Return to heat and cook, stirring constantly, until mixture thickens and comes to a boil. Remove from heat; cool. Spread small amount apricot jam in the bottom of tart shells. Spoon cherry mixture into the shells. If desired, top with whipped cream.

YIELD: 8 SERVINGS

Château de Pray

✤ ✤ ✤

BURGUNDY GRAPE PIE
Tartelettes aux Raisins Bourguignonne

2 CUPS GRAPES	1 TABLESPOON CORNSTARCH
½ CUP RED WINE	6 BAKED TART SHELLS
2 TABLESPOONS BRANDY	2 TABLESPOONS ORANGE
½ CUP SUGAR	MARMALADE

WHIPPED CREAM

Put grapes and wine into a saucepan; heat very slowly until grapes burst and seeds come to the surface. Skim the seeds. Stir in brandy. Mix together sugar and cornstarch; stir into mixture. Cook, stirring constantly, until mixture thickens and comes to a boil. Remove from heat; cool. Spread each tart with a teaspoon of the orange marmalade; divide grape mixture among the tarts. Spread tops with whipped cream.

YIELD: 6 SERVINGS

Château St. Jean

✤ ✤ ✤

LEMON SOUFFLÉ PIE

Tarte de Soufflé au Citron

3 EGGS, SEPARATED
¾ CUP SUGAR, DIVIDED
¼ CUP FIRMLY PACKED BROWN
   SUGAR
¼ TEASPOON SALT

⅓ CUP LEMON JUICE
1 TEASPOON GRATED LEMON AND
   ORANGE RIND
2 TABLESPOONS GROUND ALMONDS
1 9-INCH BAKED PASTRY SHELL

Beat egg yolks until thick and lemon-colored. Beat in ¼ cup of the sugar which has been combined with the brown sugar, salt, lemon juice, and lemon and orange rind. Place in top of double boiler. Cook over hot water, stirring constantly, until thickened, about 10 minutes. Remove from water; cool. Stir in almonds. Beat egg whites until stiff, but not dry. Gradually add remaining ½ cup sugar and beat until very stiff. Fold into lemon mixture; pile into pastry shell. Bake in a 400°F. oven, until lightly browned, about 10 to 12 minutes.

YIELD: ONE 9-INCH PIE

Château de Trigance

✤ ✤ ✤

RAISIN AND NUT PIE

Tarte aux Raisins à la Ferluche

2 CUPS RAISINS
3 CUPS BOILING WATER, DIVIDED
½ CUP SUGAR
2 TABLESPOONS CORNSTARCH
2 TABLESPOONS COLD WATER
½ TEASPOON SALT

½ TEASPOON GRATED LEMON RIND
2 TABLESPOONS LEMON JUICE
2 TEASPOONS GRATED ORANGE
   RIND
½ CUP ORANGE JUICE
1 CUP CHOPPED NUTS

1 9-INCH BAKED PASTRY SHELL

Put raisins into a saucepan. Add 1½ cups of the boiling water; let stand 5 minutes. Drain. Return raisins to saucepan and add remaining 1½ cups boiling water and sugar. Bring to a boil and cook, stirring constantly, 5 minutes. Blend together cornstarch and water; stir into raisin mixture. Cook until mixture comes to a boil and is thickened and clear. Remove from heat; stir in salt, lemon rind and juice, orange rind and juice, and nuts; mix well. Turn into prepared pastry shell. Chill.

YIELD: ONE 9-INCH PIE

Château d'Ayres

✦ ✦ ✦

HONEY HARLEQUIN PUDDING

Pouding Harlequin

1 CUP FINELY CHOPPED MIXED
   CANDIED FRUIT
½ CUP CRUMBLED MACAROONS

⅛ TEASPOON SALT
4 TABLESPOONS LIQUID HONEY
2 CUPS HEAVY CREAM, WHIPPED

Fold fruit, macaroons, salt, and honey into whipped cream; mix well.
Turn into freezer trays; freeze until firm.

YIELD: APPROXIMATELY 1 QUART

Château de Cheronnac

✦ ✦ ✦

APPLE CUSTARD PASTRY

Flan aux Pommes Pâtissière

APPLESAUCE
1 9-INCH UNBAKED PASTRY SHELL
   SIEVED APRICOT JAM
3 TO 4 POUNDS APPLES, PARED,
   CORED AND CUT IN ⅛-INCH
   THICK SLICES

MELTED BUTTER
SUGAR
MELTED CURRANT JELLY

Spread a thin layer of applesauce in bottom of pastry shell; spoon a thin
layer of jam over top. Place apples in circular fashion over the jam
filling to the top. Brush with melted butter; sprinkle with sugar. Bake
in a 425°F. oven, 15 minutes. Reduce heat to 375°F. and bake 30 minutes longer. Remove from oven; brush with currant jelly. Cool.

YIELD: ONE 9-INCH PIE

L'Oustau de Baumanière

✦ ✦ ✦

APRICOT TARTS WITH RUM À LA FRANÇAISE

Tartelettes aux Abricots au Rhum à la Française

12 BAKED TART SHELLS
⅓ CUP FIRMLY PACKED BROWN
   SUGAR
2 TABLESPOONS CORNSTARCH
   DASH SALT
1¼ CUPS CANNED APRICOT JUICE

2 TABLESPOONS MELTED BUTTER
12 CANNED APRICOT HALVES
   SIEVED APRICOT JAM
2 PACKAGES (3 OUNCES EACH)
   CREAM CHEESE
1 TABLESPOON RUM

Prepare and bake tart shells, substituting apricot juice for water. Cool.
Mix together sugar, cornstarch, and salt in a saucepan. Stir in apricot
juice. Place over medium heat and cook, stirring constantly, until mixture comes to a boil and is thickened and clear. Remove from heat; stir
in butter. Cool slightly and add apricot halves. Chill. When ready to
serve, spread small amount apricot jam in bottom of tart shells. Beat
cream cheese with rum until smooth; divide mixture among tart shells.
Spoon in apricot mixture. Top with whipped cream which has been
flavored with a small amount of almond extract.

YIELD: 12 SERVINGS

Château de la Vallée Bleue

✦ ✦ ✦

RUM PECAN TARTS

Tartelettes aux Noisettes et au Rhum

1 CUP FIRMLY PACKED BROWN
   SUGAR
½ CUP WATER
2 EGGS
2½ TABLESPOONS FLOUR
⅛ TEASPOON SALT

1 CUP MILK
2 TABLESPOONS BUTTER
1 TEASPOON VANILLA
2 TABLESPOONS RUM
6 DOZEN PECAN HALVES
12 UNBAKED TART SHELLS

Put sugar and water into a saucepan. Place over low heat, stirring occasionally until sugar dissolves. Boil over medium heat 5 minutes or until a
medium thick syrup forms. Beat eggs in top of double boiler. Stir in
flour and salt. Add milk and cook, stirring constantly, until mixture
thickens. Remove from water; stir in butter, vanilla, half the sugar syrup
and rum; mix well. Divide among the tart shells; top each with 6 pecan
halves. Pour remaining sugar syrup over top. Bake in a 450°F. oven,
12 to 15 minutes. Cool. Garnish with whipped cream.

YIELD: 12 SERVINGS

Château de Mercuès

✦ ✦ ✦

BABA AU RHUM
Baba au Rhum

1 PACKAGE DRY YEAST
¼ CUP LUKEWARM WATER
4 EGGS, BEATEN
2 CUPS SIFTED ALL-PURPOSE FLOUR

⅓ CUP MELTED BUTTER, COOLED
1½ TABLESPOONS SUGAR
¼ TEASPOON SALT

Sprinkle yeast on warm water until dissolved. Add with beaten eggs to flour mixture; beat 5 minutes. Cover and let stand in a warm place 35 minutes. Add butter, sugar, and salt to dough; beat well. Turn out on a lightly floured surface and knead 10 minutes (mixture will not hold together at first). Turn into a greased tube pan. Cover and let rise in a warm place until double in bulk. Bake in a 375°F. oven, 45 minutes. Loosen while warm from sides of pan and invert on a cake rack. Serve with Rum Sauce.

RUM SAUCE
Sauce au Rhum

1 CUP SUGAR
½ CUP WATER

DASH SALT
½ CUP RUM

Put sugar, water, and salt in a saucepan. Cook over low heat, stirring constantly, until sugar is dissolved. Bring to a boil; boil 2 minutes. Remove from heat; cool. When almost cold, stir in rum. Place inverted baba on serving platter. Carefully spoon sauce over surface, allowing small amount to drip into the platter to be soaked up by the crust. Let stand 1 hour; turn baba right side up.

Note: If desired baba may be baked in greased custard cups. Fill cups half way with dough and let rise until double in bulk. Bake in a 400°F. oven, 25 minutes.

Château St. Jean

✤ ✤ ✤

FRIED PANCAKES *Pannequets Frits*

5 TABLESPOONS FLOUR
2 TABLESPOONS SUGAR
1 EGG

3 EGG YOLKS
⅛ TEASPOON VANILLA
MILK

Mix together flour and sugar; beat in egg, egg yolks, and vanilla and mix to a smooth paste. Gradually add enough milk to obtain a liquid paste, thick enough to cover the bowl of a tablespoon when turned upside down. Drop 3 tablespoons of the batter into a buttered, large light skillet, tilting pan to cover bottom entirely. When brown underneath, turn and cook other side. Transfer to a large round platter. Sprinkle with 1 teaspoon kirsch, rum, or brandy, and spread with favorite jelly. Roll as for a jelly roll; cut on a slant into 1-inch pieces. Dip in slightly beaten egg, then in sieved macaroon or cake crumbs. Deep-fry at 390°F., 1 minute, or until crisp brown. Repeat. Sprinkle with confectioners sugar and serve with Hard Sauce.*

YIELD: 4 SERVINGS

*See page 147

Château St. Jean

✤ ✤ ✤

FRIED PANCAKES WITH ALMONDS *Pannequets aux Amandes*

1 TABLESPOON MELTED BUTTER
1 DOZEN ALMONDS, FINELY
  GROUND

2 BITTER ALMONDS, FINELY
  GROUND
2 TEASPOONS CONFECTIONERS
  SUGAR

Prepare batter for Pannequets Frits.* To the batter add butter, almonds, and sugar. Follow directions for cooking and serve as pancakes or deep-fry.

YIELD: 4 SERVINGS

* See above

Hostellerie du Prieuré

✤ ✤ ✤

CHOCOLATE MARSHMALLOW MERINGUE

Meringue au Chocolat

16 MARSHMALLOWS, QUARTERED
1 TABLESPOON MILK
2 EGG WHITES
¼ CUP SUGAR
⅛ TEASPOON SALT

1 TABLESPOON UNSWEETENED
COCOA POWDER
1 9-INCH SQUARE BAKED WHITE
OR YELLOW CAKE LAYER
CHOCOLATE BISCUIT GLACE*

Place marshmallows and milk in a saucepan over very low heat. Heat, stirring constantly, until marshmallows are almost melted. Remove from heat and beat until a smooth, fluffy mixture is formed. Cool. Beat egg whites until stiff, but not dry. Gradually add sugar and salt and beat until very stiff. Fold in cocoa. Fold into marshmallow mixture. Place cake layer on a baking sheet; invert frozen Chocolate Biscuit Glace on top. Cover top and sides with meringue. Bake in a 475°F. oven, a few minutes, or until delicately browned. Serve immediately.

YIELD: 9 TO 12 SERVINGS

*See page 131

Le Prieuré

✤ ✤ ✤

MERINGUE COOKIES VALENCE

Valenciennes

5 TABLESPOONS BUTTER OR
MARGARINE
1 CUP SIFTED CONFECTIONERS
SUGAR
3 EGG YOLKS
½ TEASPOON ALMOND EXTRACT
½ TEASPOON VANILLA

1 CUP SIFTED CAKE FLOUR
3 TEASPOONS BAKING POWDER
¼ TEASPOON SALT
DASH GROUND GINGER
1 CUP FLAKED COCONUT
3 CUPS TOASTED CRUMBLED
MACAROONS

2 EGG WHITES

Cream butter until light and fluffy; gradually blend in sugar. Beat in egg yolks one at a time. Stir in flavorings. Sift in flour, baking powder, salt, and ginger; mix well. Stir in coconut and macaroons. Beat egg whites until stiff, but not dry; fold into mixture. Drop by teaspoonfuls on a greased baking sheet spreading thin, 3 inches apart. Bake in a 425°F. oven, 5 minutes, or until firm and lightly browned.

YIELD: APPROXIMATELY 3 DOZEN COOKIES

Château de la Vallée Bleue

✦ ✦ ✦

FROSTED HALF MOONS

Demi-lunes Lyonnaises

2½ CUPS SIFTED ALL-PURPOSE
    FLOUR
¼ CUP SUGAR
¼ TEASPOON SALT

1 CUP BUTTER
⅔ CUP GRATED SEMI-SWEET
    CHOCOLATE
1 CUP TOASTED ALMONDS,
    FINELY CHOPPED

Sift together flour, sugar, and salt into a mixing bowl. Cut in butter with 2 knives or a pastry blender, until mixture resembles coarse meal. Stir in chocolate and almonds; mix well. Roll out on a lightly floured surface; cut with a crescent cooky cutter. Place on greased cooky sheet. Bake in a 325°F. oven, 18 to 20 minutes. Cool and frost with Golden Icing.

YIELD: APPROXIMATELY 4 DOZEN COOKIES

GOLDEN ICING

Glace de Sucre Dorée

2 CUPS SUGAR
½ CUP WATER
4 EGG YOLKS
    DASH SALT

½ TEASPOON GRATED ORANGE
    RIND
1 TEASPOON ORANGE JUICE
2 TO 3 TABLESPOONS LIGHT CREAM

Put sugar and water in a saucepan. Place over low heat, stirring constantly, until sugar is dissolved. Boil over medium heat until mixture reaches 250°F. on a candy thermometer. Beat egg yolks with salt until thick and lemon colored. Pour in syrup in a stream, beating constantly. Beat until cool and of a fudge consistency. Beat in orange rind, juice, and enough cream a make a spreading consistency.

Château de Creissels

✦ ✦ ✦

FRIED COOKIES

Vanités

3 EGGS
1 TABLESPOON SUGAR

1 TABLESPOON RUM OR WATER
    ALL-PURPOSE FLOUR

Beat eggs; add sugar and rum. Stir in enough flour to make a stiff dough. Knead 2 minutes. Roll out dough very thin on a lightly floured surface. Tear into pieces (do not cut with a cookie cutter). Deep-fry at 385°F., 2 minutes, or until lightly browned. Drain on absorbent paper; sift confectioners' sugar over *Vanités*.

Desserts • 143

Château Choiseul

✦ ✦ ✦

STEAMED CHOCOLATE FRUIT LOAVES, FRENCH MANNER

Gâteau de Chocolat aux Fruits

½ CUP EACH RAISINS AND
  CURRANTS
½ CUP EACH FINELY CHOPPED
  CITRON, ANGELICA, CANDIED
  ORANGE PEEL, GREEN
  MARASCHINO CHERRIES
¼ CUP FINELY CHOPPED
  CANDIED PINEAPPLE
½ CUP FINELY CHOPPED
  FILBERTS OR HAZELNUTS
1⅔ CUPS SIFTED CAKE FLOUR
⅓ CUP POWDERED COCOA
1 TEASPOON BAKING SODA
⅛ TEASPOON SALT

1 TEASPOON CINNAMON
¾ TEASPOON ALLSPICE
½ TEASPOON EACH GROUND
  CLOVES, MACE, AND GINGER
½ CUP BUTTER
½ CUP FIRMLY PACKED BROWN
  SUGAR
½ CUP GRANULATED SUGAR
½ TEASPOON ALMOND EXTRACT
1 TEASPOON GRATED ORANGE
  RIND
2 EGGS
½ CUP MOLASSES
¾ CUP SOUR MILK

¼ CUP RUM

Put fruits and nuts into a large mixing bowl. Sift in flour, cocoa, soda, salt, and spices. Mix well with fruit and nut mixture. Cream butter; gradually add sugars and cream until light and fluffy. Blend in almond extract and orange rind. Add eggs, one at a time, beating well after each addition. Blend in molasses. Add floured fruit and nut mixture alternately with the sour milk; stir in rum. Turn into 2 greased and floured 9 x 5 x 3-inch loaf pans. Cover tops tightly with heavy-duty aluminum foil; secure with string. Place on rack in a deep kettle. Pour in boiling water to slightly more than half the depth of pans. Cover. Steam 3 hours. Cool 40 minutes. Unwrap and cool completely. Store in a covered crock jar 1 month before slicing.

YIELD: 2 LOAVES

Hostellerie de la Poste

⚜ ⚜ ⚜

SWEETNESS OF LIFE

Douceur de Vivre

7 EGG WHITES
1 CUP SUGAR
1 CUP BUTTER, MELTED
4 TABLESPOONS KIRSCH, DIVIDED

4 TABLESPOONS CURAÇAO, DIVIDED
1 POUND CAKE
CONFECTIONERS' SUGAR ICING
FLAVORED WITH KIRSCH

Warm the egg whites and sugar in a saucepan. Remove from heat and beat until completely cool. Add melted butter. Stir until well blended. Divide this mixture into two bowls. In first bowl add half the kirsch. In the second bowl add half the curaçao. Slice the pound cake lengthwise into three slices. Sprinkle one slice with remaining kirsch and spread with kirsch mixture. Sprinkle second slice with remaining curaçao; place on top of first slice and spread with curaçao mixture. Top with third slice. Spread with icing.

Le Prieuré

⚜ ⚜ ⚜

FRENCH TWELFTH CAKE

Petites Galettes du Curé

1 CUP RAISINS, PLUMPED AND
CHOPPED
2 CUPS FINELY CHOPPED
TOASTED ALMONDS
1½ CUPS SIFTED ALL-PURPOSE
FLOUR

¼ TEASPOON SALT
1 CUP SUGAR
1 TEASPOON BAKING POWDER
½ TEASPOON CINNAMON
3 EGGS, WELL BEATEN

Mix together raisins and almonds in a mixing bowl. Sift in flour, salt, sugar, baking powder, and cinnamon. Blend in eggs; mix well. Roll out on lightly floured surface; cut with cooky cutter into 2-inch rounds. Place on baking sheets lined with greased aluminum foil. Bake in a 325°F. oven, 15 to 20 minutes. Cool 1 to 2 minutes before removing.

YIELD: APPROXIMATELY 4 DOZEN

Château de Creissels

✣ ✣ ✣

RED DEVIL CAKE
Gâteau du Diable

2 CUPS SIFTED CAKE FLOUR
¼ TEASPOON SALT
1¼ TEASPOONS BAKING SODA
½ CUP BUTTER
1 CUP SUGAR

2 EGGS
2 SQUARES UNSWEETENED MELTED
CHOCOLATE
1 TEASPOON VANILLA
¾ CUP BUTTERMILK

⅓ CUP BOILING WATER

Sift together flour, salt, and baking soda. Cream butter; gradually add sugar. Cream until light and fluffy. Beat in eggs one at a time, blend in melted chocolate and vanilla. Add flour mixture alternately with butter-milk, beginning and ending with flour. Gradually add boiling water and beat until blended. Turn into 2 greased and floured 8-inch round layer cake pans. Bake in a 375°F. oven, 25 to 30 minutes. Cool. Frost with favorite frosting.

YIELD: ONE 8-INCH LAYER CAKE

Château de Divonne

✣ ✣ ✣

STRAWBERRY CAKE
Gâteau aux Fraises

1 QUART STRAWBERRIES
1 CUP SUGAR
⅛ TEASPOON SALT
2 TEASPOONS LEMON JUICE

1 ENVELOPE UNFLAVORED GELATIN
½ CUP WATER
1 CUP HEAVY CREAM, WHIPPED
2 DOZEN VANILLA WAFERS

Wash, hull, and slice strawberries; place in a deep bowl. Sprinkle with sugar, salt, and lemon juice. Let stand 1 hour, stirring occasionally. Sprinkle gelatin on water in a saucepan to soften; place over medium heat, stirring constantly, until gelatin is dissolved. Remove from heat; strain in cold strawberry juice. Fold in whipped cream; fold in strawberries. Layer strawberry mixture alternately with vanilla wafers in a wax-paper lined loaf pan, beginning and ending with strawberry mixture. Chill in refrigerator overnight, or freeze 2 hours. Invert on serving platter, garnish top with additional sweetened whipped cream. Mixture will be semi-frozen.

YIELD: 8 TO 10 SERVINGS

Château de Mimont

✦ ✦ ✦

FRENCH CHERRY LAYER CAKE *Gâteau aux Cerises à la Française*

2 CUPS SIFTED CAKE FLOUR
2 TEASPOONS BAKING POWDER
½ TEASPOON SALT
½ CUP BUTTER

1¼ CUPS SUGAR
1 TABLESPOON KIRSCH
⅔ CUP MILK
4 EGG WHITES

Sift together flour, baking powder, and salt. Cream butter. Gradually add sugar. Cream until light and fluffy. Blend in kirsch. Add sifted dry ingredients alternately with milk beginning and ending with flour. Beat egg whites until stiff, but not dry. Fold into batter. Turn into 2 greased and floured 9-inch layer cake pans. Bake in a 375°F. oven, 25 to 30 minutes. Cool. Frost with Cherry Icing.

YIELD: ONE 9-INCH CAKE

CHERRY ICING *Cerises Glacées*

2 EGG WHITES
1½ CUPS SUGAR
⅛ TEASPOON SALT
⅛ TEASPOON CREAM OF TARTAR
½ CUP CHOPPED ALMONDS

⅓ CUP WHITE WINE
½ TEASPOON ALMOND EXTRACT
⅓ CUP CHOPPED MARASCHINO
CHERRIES

Put egg whites, sugar, salt, cream of tartar, and wine in top of double boiler. Place over boiling water and beat with rotary or electric beater, until frosting holds its shape, 5 to 7 minutes. Remove from water; beat in almond extract. Add cherries and almonds to ⅓ of the frosting; spread between the cake layers. Frost top and sides of cake with remaining frosting.

✦ ✦ ✦

HARD SAUCE *Crème au Beurre*

½ CUP SWEET BUTTER, SOFT
½ CUP CONFECTIONERS' SUGAR

⅛ TEASPOON VANILLA

Cream butter. Slowly add sugar and vanilla, blending well.

COFFEE SAUCE MOUSSELINE

Crème Mousseline au Café

3 EGG YOLKS
1 TABLESPOON INSTANT COFFEE
  DASH SALT

3 TABLESPOONS BRANDY
½ CUP SUGAR
1 CUP HEAVY CREAM, WHIPPED

Beat egg yolks until light and lemon-colored with coffee, salt, and brandy. Gradually beat in the sugar. Place in top of double boiler and cook, over hot water, stirring constantly, 5 minutes. Remove from heat; cool. Fold in heavy cream.

YIELD: APPROXIMATELY 2½ CUPS

✢ ✢ ✢

PUFF PASTE

Pâte Feuillté

½ POUND BUTTER
2 CUPS SIFTED ALL-PURPOSE
  FLOUR

½ TEASPOON SALT
½ CUP ICE COLD WATER

Knead butter until all water is extracted. Cut 2 tablespoons of the butter into the flour which has been combined with salt. Knead five minutes. Roll out ¼ inch thick, keeping paste rectangular and corners square. Place remaining butter in center of lower half of dough; cover with upper half and fold right side under and left side over. Roll to ¼ inch thickness. Repeat this process 4 times. Refrigerate 1 hour. Cut into desired shapes. Bake in a 450°F. oven, 5 minutes. Reduce heat to 375°F. and bake 25 to 30 minutes longer.

✢ ✢ ✢

PIE PASTRY

Pâte à Foncer

2 CUPS SIFTED ALL-PURPOSE FLOUR
1 TEASPOON SALT

1 CUP SHORTENING
¼ CUP ICE WATER

Combine flour and salt. Cut in shortening with two knives or pastry blender. Add water all at once, tossing mixture with a fork to distribute water evenly. Press dough together into 2 equal-sized balls. Chill for 10 minutes. Roll on lightly floured board or pastry cloth to ⅛-inch thickness. Fit carefully, without stretching, into pie plate. To bake shells, bake at 450°F. for 12 to 15 minutes.

YIELD: PASTRY FOR TWO 8-INCH PIE SHELLS

Châteaux

CHÂTEAU D'ARTIGNY

A view which has gladdened the sight of man for eight and a half centuries.

With its gardens and its chapel site laid out as replicas of those at Versailles, the magnificent Château d'Artigny of today bears a striking similarity to the splendors of the Royal Château. The park is landscaped to match the magnificence of the grounds surrounding the hundreds of other historical castles, medieval houses, and palatial residences near the legendary towns of Loches, Tours, and Chinon in the Loire Valley, playground of French kings from the fourteenth to the seventeenth centuries. Every element in this luxurious accommodation was designed to rival these places in beauty and elegance.

In our times the great antiquary and interior decorator, Scapula, has taken up where the artisans of yesteryear left off. The rooms of colored marble which Monsieur Coty, celebrated perfumer and builder of the present structure, designated on the top floor of his palace as kitchens, pastry kitchens, linen, laundry, and pot-washing rooms are now gorgeous bedchambers filled with priceless antiques. The dressing room of Madame Coty—with its private staircase and its seventy-eight wardrobe closets, its ivory inlaid woods, and its handsome mosaic floor—has been divided to make five bedrooms, but its beauties have remained unmarred. Cheeses ripen today in the special vault built to preserve the furs of Madame Coty and her guests. And in the corridors, constructed to conduct the air currents of Coty's early attempts at air conditioning, vintage wines are stored.

The history of this, France's most opulent château-hotel, is linked with that of the great builder and enigmatic warrior, Foulques Nerra. This lavish, violent, unscrupulous, sometimes penitent lord directed the construction of bastions, churches, monasteries, ramparts, and dungeons throughout Touraine and Angers. One of these edifices, the fortress of Esvres and Montbazon, built in 1123 as the residence of the commander at Montbazon, was designed to protect the Indre Valley from invasion by the "Barbarians from Tours."

In the fifteenth century this fortress became the property of Jean d'Artennes and the lands became known as the "Puy d'Artigny" (Peak of Artigny). The site still presents one of the most seductively beautiful scenes along the Indre. In 1769, one of its owners, Luc René Testard of Bournais, treasurer to King Louis XV, built an elegant château on the "Puy."

The château remained untouched by the ravages of the Revolution. It stood undisturbed until 1910 when, charmed by the site and dreaming of an imposing "royal" palace, François Coty acquired the Puy d'Artigny and ordered the ancient château razed. He retained the most gifted architects and artisans to replace the old structure with his own dream. The results of their craftsmanship have been carefully preserved.

In the sumptuous upstairs rotunda, one can savor the spirit and gaiety of Hoffbauer's astonishing fresco *trompe-l'oeil,* "Costume Ball at the Château," and through tall, gilt-framed windows one can look out from the Puy d'Artigny upon the same rare view of the Indre Valley which has gladdened the sight of man for eight and a half centuries.

151

CHÂTEAU D'AYRES

Ancient traditions of the French lords preserved.

Meyrueis—home of the Château d'Ayres in the south of France—is a small village nestled between the Jonte Canyon and the base of steep-rising calcareous table lands called *les causses*. From this center of geological marvels one can visit the grotto of Dargilan; the Armand Chasm with its immense underground gallery of glittering stalactites; Montpellier-le-Vieux, remarkable array of shaped rocks; the subterranean river of Bramabian; and the spectacular Canyon of the Tarn.

The town itself is ancient, being part of lands inhabited more than fifteen hundred years ago by the Visigoths.

In 1034 Bermont, brother of the Count of Carcassone, presented the Parish of Meyrueis to the Abbey of St. Guilhem-le-Desert. Founded by the pious monk, who was the lifetime companion of Emperor Charlemagne, this Abbey possessed a church which is today the repository of an important religious relic—a wooden piece of the "true cross," focal point of veneration each year, on May 3rd.

In the twelfth century the structure known as Château d'Ayres was built in the form of a Benedictine monastery. The monks who inhabited it were exceedingly greedy and legend has it that the peasants, tiring of their poverty, rose up one night and set fire to the castle. The monks ran out into the darkness, leaving behind their hidden treasure, which has never been located. Evidences of such a conflagration are still visible on the foundations of the Château d'Ayres. Put to fire at the end of the twelfth century, the monastery never regained its importance.

We know that Meyrueis was once the dowry of Isabelle de Roquefeuil, an ancestor of the Rockefeller families of America. Acquiring the town in 1230, she joined it to the properties of the powerful Counts of Rodez, of whom we shall read again in the histories of Château de Cresseils and Château de Lévezou.

The lands of the monastery were parceled and, after 1303, the château was purchased by the intrepid warrior Guillaume de Nogaret, Chancellor under Philippe Le Bel. Charged with the duty of stopping Pope Boniface VIII at Anagni, De Nogaret did not fear to use violence even against the Pontiff. His coat-of-arms is still above the fireplaces of Château d'Ayres.

About 1600, the Sire of Ayres and Meyrueis, a powerful Protestant chieftan, came to destroy the Convent of Lanourgne. The name of the château stems from this event, although it is not known whether the Sire ever inhabited the castle, which remained in the De Nogaret family until the present century.

In 1922 the château was purchased by the parents of its current hostess, Madame Teissier du Cros. (Romantically enough when Monsieur Teissier du Cros, a descendant of the De Nogaret family, came to ask for the hand of Madame in marriage, he recognized the grounds where he had played as a child.)

Beginning with two guest chambers in 1924, the château was brought to a state of perfection by 1940. During World War II its interior was desecrated, but since then Monsieur and Madame Teissier du Cros have succeeded in restoring the castle to its former grandeur. Guests of the château are encouraged to enter the kitchen where they may pay proper respect to the artistry of the chef. Thus the ancient traditions of French lords are perpetuated at the Château d'Ayres.

153

L'OUSTAU DE BAUMANIÈRE

Pure luxury found on the scene of the great Princes of Orange who traced their lineage from Balthazar of the Three Wise Men.

Baumanière was built as an olive-oil mill four hundred years ago in the foot-hills of the Alpilles. It stands at the entrance to the Valley of the Inferno, said to be the inspiration for Dante's epic work. Situated below Les Baux-en Provence, in the Vale of the Fountain, this lovely property was made into a hostelry in 1946 and has become a world-famous dining spot.

From Baumanière one can see the ancient *Cité,* a medieval city which once teemed with the activities of the royal court of the Princes of Orange. These Lords of Les Baux traced their lineage from Balthazar of the Three Wise Men. They displayed their fierce pride by placing the star of the nativity, with its sixteen rays, on their own coat-of-arms.

To reach the present-day towering ruin one must climb on foot to its rocky entrance. Built in the tenth century, at a time when the great Lords possessed seventy-nine estates, Les Baux once boasted a population of six thousand. Its stone walls sheltered the troubadours of the Middle Ages. Today narrow streets beckon us to explore the vestiges of elegant medieval life: a feudal gate bearing the crest of the First Marquis of Les Baux; mansions of the fourteenth, fifteenth, and sixteenth centuries with magnificent crossbar windows; the ruins of the Re-formed Protestant Temple; the Church of St. Vincent, still standing with its Roman-Byzantine detail and its crypt, which protects the remains of the proud lords and ladies.

Each Christmas, a midnight mass called the "Festival of the Shepards" is celebrated by torchlight at Les Baux. The personages of the Nativity come alive to recount, in ancient fashion and dress, the tale of the Magi.

From high on the ramparts of the Saracen Tower in Les Baux, the eye sweeps across the Marsh of Fos. Across the plains of the Camargue the blue crescent of the Mediterranean, almost thirty miles away, can be seen on the horizon. To the west spreads the Vale of the Fountain sheltering the flower-encircled Oustau de Baumanière.

Nearby is the Cupola of Queen Joan. Its Renaissance architecture inspires images of the tender rendezvous which took place under its graceful arches before the murder of its beauteous builder.

Under the administration of the Manville family, Les Baux became an im-portant center of Protestantism. Their handsome sixteenth-century mansion, restored by the Beaux Arts,* is now used as a town hall and is the center of government for the two hundred and fifty faithful inhabitants who remain. Some of the outstanding painters, poets, and artisans of Provence, and of all France, have come to take up residence amid the rare and rugged fascinations of Les Baux to seek fresh inspiration.

On leaving the *Cité* one carries away a vision of a medieval world. Lost in a reverie of disbelief, the traveler strolls down the rocky hill to a contrasting world of modern serenity which awaits at the gates of L'Oustau de Baumanière.

*The Beaux Arts is the National Institute of Fine Arts which controls and records all objects of authentic historic beauty and classifies them according to their place in antiquity.

CHÂTEAU DE BETZ

One of the most beautiful parks in France, yet it is only one hour from Paris. Cordial and elegant atmosphere.

Every romantic fairy tale begins with the words, "Once upon a time a lovely princess fell in love with a handsome prince." So begins the tale of the Château de Betz, its park classified by the Beaux Arts as "one of the most beautiful sites of France." For many centuries the property was the feudal domain of the Lords of Betz and Crépy, but in the eighteenth century Betz was purchased by the passionate Princess of Monaco, Marie Catherine de Brignole.

Born in Genoa, Marie met Honoré Grimaldi III when she was six and by sixteen was desperately in love with him. Married to this opportunistic cavalier who was her mother's paramour, she was soon abandoned by him for the excitements of the court and the hunt. To further his own career Honoré summoned Marie to the court, where she was noticed by the Prince de Condé. When their flirtation finally came to Honoré's attention, the Princess fled to the country and finally to a convent at Mans to escape his despotic rantings and continued neglect. Ultimately, in 1770, she was granted a divorce. Honoré was so outraged that he nullified her title and forbade her to see her sons.

The Princess, in compensation, threw herself into the gaiety of court life, becoming the acknowledged mistress of the Prince de Condé. She purchased Betz, close to Condé's magnificent property at Chantilly, and dispensed four million dollars for furnishings and gardens.

Her château, demolished in 1810, was situated on an island in the river which still winds placidly through the park. On a second island, reached by a beautiful Chinese bridge, was an oriental kiosk. In the center of the meadow there stands a grove of trees which once sheltered the Princess' private baths. In the same field are the remains of the Column of Tancredi bearing Voltaire's emblem:

Preserve my motto; it is dear to my heart.
These words are sacred to me: they are Love and Honor.

Along the paths a Druid temple, a mill, a pavilion of repose, and an orangery once stood. Today one finds only the remains of the twelfth-century castle, the obelisk commemorating American Independence, and the Valley of the Tombs. Downstream is a lovely medieval chapel, the Grand Waterfall, and the "Temple of Friendship." This model of Greco-Roman Renaissance art was the trysting place of the Princess of Monaco and her lover. Their intimate apartment on the second floor remains for all to visit.

The Temple contains statues by Stouf (originals now in the Louvre), and a casting by Pigalle entitled "Love and Friendship," for which Madame de Pompadour posed. On its base is this quatrain:

Wise Friendship, Love looks for your presence once again.
Captivated by your sweetness, captivated by your fidelity,
It comes to beg you to adorn its fetters
With all the virtues that are thine.

Eventually reverses caused the Prince de Condé to flee to England. Marie followed and upon the death of Honoré, she waited to become Princess de Condé. Thirteen years passed before her lover fulfilled her hopes and married her in 1808. Her joy was short-lived, for in 1813 the beautiful Princess died in the arms of the lover and husband with whom she had shared the exquisite intimacy of the Château de Betz.

LA CARDINALE

A charming and quiet place combining excellent food and beautiful rooms.

The setting of La Cardinale is a quiet quay shaded by tall Italian poplars along the Rhône River. This famed hostelry stands in the ancient village of Baix. Classified by the Beaux Arts, its historic beauty may never be changed.

Founded as a Phoenician trading post, Baix later became a way station for bargemen and in the twelfth century its strategic location made it the perfect site for a river fortress. An imposing stronghold was built, possessing six great circular towers. Later, during the Religious Wars, these imposing towers were struck down by an ordinance of Cardinal Richelieu. (A vestige of one tower remains in the salon of the present hotel.)

Enigmatically, the Cardinal himself, with his prisoners Cinq Mars and de Thou, stopped as a guest in this very house. Extremely ill, and borne on a litter, he left a few days later on a barge. Carried upriver to Lyon, he directed the execution of these two men who had plotted against him. In gratitude for the attentions of his host at Baix he sent a painting to grace the room in which he had slept. This picture, "The Martyrdom of St. Sabastian," now hangs in the museum of Aix-en-Provence.

The name of the house dates from Cardinal Richelieu's visit. The inner structure is the oldest part. Built upon the original fortifications, it contains an interesting crypt. The handsomest feature of this house is the authentic Louis XIII door, which opens out upon the charming main street of Baix. Of heavy oak, perfectly preserved, its raised diamond-shaped carvings bear the patina of centuries.

In the sixteenth century a Scot, remembered only as Gordon, married a girl from Baix. Deciding to settle in the region, he retained an architect to transform the old house and create the elegant atmosphere which is still preserved at La Cardinale. His descendents eventually moved across the river and today the opulent Château de Lagarde (a French form of the name Gordon) still dominates the opposite bank of the Rhône within hailing distance of its proprietor's ancestral home, La Cardinale.

For a short while during the seventeenth century La Cardinale housed the mayors of Baix and the names and heraldic shields of these administrators may still be seen on the staircase of the hostelry.

The house passed into the famous family of Orange, Suarez d'Aulan, but its present owners, Monsieur and Madame Marcel Tilloy (known best by their theatrical names, Nelly Nell and Marc Duthyl), acquired it from their friend and colleague, Madame Grégoire, former danseuse in the ballet of the Moulin Rouge in Paris.

The rooms of La Cardinale were at one time decorated with the vivid posters of Toulouse Lautrec but, though every effort was made to save them, these masterpieces had to be destroyed when renovations of the house were made.

In 1952, Madam Tilloy converted La Cardinale into a hostelry and, due largely to her culinary artistry, its reputation has spread to scores of artists, musicians, writers, and gastronomes.

CHÂTEAU DE LA CAZE

A most architecturally striking châteaux.

The present Château de La Caze, under the control of the Beaux Arts, completely preserves its medieval character. Its crossbar windows, its great chimneys of stone, its unique cobblestone corridors gleaming from the footfalls of generations of inhabitants, the apartment of Soubeyrane Alamand with its canopied bed—these attest to the tastefulness and love with which this castle was constructed in 1489. Unlike other châteaux of its era, La Caze was not built for military purposes. It was designed as a honeymoon haven.

In those days the nearby town of St. Enimie possessed a celebrated monastery of which François Alamand was Prior. Among his private estates was the domain of Château de Grandlac, still in existence. This property extended to the bottom of the beautiful gorge which walls the banks of the River Tarn. The sight so enthralled the Prior's niece, Soubeyrane Alamand (at the time engaged to Sir Monclar), that she asked for this lovely point of land jutting from the rock. It had a fresh, cool spring tumbling down into the river. Defying tradition, Soubeyrane built her dream house at the bottom of the gorge. She constructed her château in order to escape the icy winds and deep winter snow of the surrounding heights, preferring the warmth of the sun and the year-round accessibility of the river.

The Alamand lineage ended with Soubeyrane and the châteaux of Grandlac and La Caze were inherited by the Mostuéjouls. With this great family began the epoch in which the name of La Caze is linked with the golden legends of the Gorges du Tarn.

Bertrand de Mostuéjouls was a valiant swordsman known as Captain La Caze. A lieutenant for the King, we find his *nom de guerre* mentioned frequently in history where he is identified as a formidable warrior in the Wars of Religion. Abandoned with a weak army by his superior, Sire of St. Vidal, Captain La Caze substituted his own valor for that lacking in his troops. He stopped Merle, the Huguenot, from his forays at the lower end of the Tarn, preserved the surrounding territory, and reconquered the larger part of the Gevaudan region.

Bertrand's daughter was the mother of the eight famous Demoiselles de la Caze whose portraits still adorn a room of the great south tower. According to legend, they return to the gardens of the castle each night to await the lovers of their youth. Their portraits on wood, ravaged by time, give only a hint of their fabled beauty.

Since the Revolution the château has changed masters many times, but its striking architecture remains unsullied by the centuries. The realization of a romantic dream, La Caze is the first château to have been transformed into a hotel. Until 1905, when the road of the Gorges du Tarn was opened, paying guests could only reach the castle by boat.

Still a great cube of glistening pink stone in a verdant setting, its impressive square donjon rising above the drawbridge, La Caze is as lovely now as on the day Soubeyrane Alamand came to live there as a bride.

CHÂTEAU DE CHALLES

A comfortable, pleasant hotel with a glorious view of the Alpes.

This fortified house and its village bear the name of a powerful family of knights who possessed many fiefs in the twelfth century. A De Challes is mentioned as a principal participant in the tournaments at Chambery as early as 1348.

The De Challes Château was originally situated on the high ground above the village; but preferring a more accessible site, the family built another château lower down the mountain, though it still dominates the plains. The new castle had three semicircular towers, a lovely dining room with a chapel leading from it, well-furnished rooms decorated with paintings, and a library. In addition to the main house there was a square tower of three floors (now the Grand Hotel) and an orangery, stable, and press. All these structures later became the nucleus of the thermal establishment which we visit today.

The knights of Challes held complete jurisdiction of the commune and occupied the château until 1590 when, with the death of Louis de Challes, governor of Bourg-en-Bresse, the property was ceded to Louis Milliet, Baron of Faverges, Grand Chancellor and ambassador of the Duke of Savoy. The Baron made Château de Challes his preferred residence and soon took its name as his own. A great reformer of finance and justice, he was the father of Hector de Challes, who was responsible for elevating the property to a Barony in 1618. President of the Senate, ambassador of the court of Henry IV, Hector had nineteen children, the oldest of whom became president of the Chamber of Accounts and received the title of Marquis de Challes in 1669. Baron Hector's other children also had brilliant careers. One of them, a Jesuit teacher who was summoned to Paris by Louis XIV, left his name on a great mathematical treatise. Other sons were honored as ambassadors, financiers, senators, high churchmen, and distinquished military men. (We also know that Jean Jacques Rousseau gave music lessons to a Mademoiselle Gaspardine Balthazarde de Challes at this time.)

The third and last Marquis de Challes died in 1777 without descendants, leaving the château to his cousins, the Faverge branch of the Milliet family. However, the Faverges did not have time to profit from their new acquisition. They were soon fleeing the onslaught of the Revolution.

Sold as a national possession, the château was purchased by Balmain, a lawyer, and one of the former managing directors to the Marquis.

One of Maître Balmain's daughters married Doctor Domenget, a physician and professor of medicine, chemistry, and botany, who (on April 11, 1841) discovered the famous spring of sulphurous waters which he named after the château. For thirty-two years Doctor Domenget and his colleagues experimented until finally, in 1873, the spring was "captured" to supply baths for a thermal station. Two years later the château itself was converted to accomodate the multitude who came seeking the benefit of the springs. Its success as a thermal establishment was so great that the nearby village, known through the centuries as Triviers, voted to change its name to Challes-les-Eaux.

Thus, by a curious turn of events, the family name of de Challes, extinct for three hundred years, came to be perpetuated by the town grown around its ancient feudal properties and by the present day Château de Challes.

163

CHÂTEAU DE CHERONNAC

Serenity in the remote countryside of France where the ancient
arts and crafts are still preserved.

Replete with the most luxurious modern adaptations for comfort, the Château de Cheronnac has been created by the imagination and charm of two of France's most attractive and well-known theatrical personalities, Lily Fayol, star of *Annie du Far West* (*Annie Get Your Gun*), and André Claveau, great recording artist, who are the proprietors of this charming hotel-restaurant. Located in the hub of France, the Château de Cheronnac is near the porcelain and enamel center of Limoges, the tapestry center of Aubusson, and the glove center of St. Junien. It is a short drive from the great Château de Rochechouart, an ancient castle perpetuating the memory of one of France's most illustrious families, which has been converted to an archaeological museum.

The château is in a region where every seven years, on the Sunday following Easter, a traditional folklore festival is celebrated. Relics of the Patron Saints of Haute-Vienne and La Creuse in their artfully contrived gold casks are venerated by the faithful. Picturesque processions wind through the flower-strewn streets. Dressed in sumptuous ancient costumes, the paraders hold aloft their colorful banners. They promenade, escorted by honor guards arranged in corps according to their trades, and accompanied by fanfares of trumpets and drums. The next such festival will be held in 1967.

Today the elegant eighteenth-century Château de Cherronac provides the traveler with the serenity of remote countryside living in an atmosphere in which the ancient arts and crafts of France are still preserved.

CHÂTEAU DE LA CHÈVRE D'OR

*A blend of medieval and provincial atmospheres created high above
the Côte d'Azur.*

The medieval city of Eze Village is the location of the Château de la Chèvre d'Or. On a solitary peak above the Côte d'Azur its curved tile roofs are bathed in the southern sun and the ancient village is like a spot of bright color against the blues of the sky and of the Mediterranean.

Eze was inhabited alternately by the people of Greece and Italy, by the Phoenicians, the Celts, and the Ligures, who lived there in 700 B.C. The latter— hearty, robust, hard-working, and jealous of their independence—formed the basis of the Provençal character as we know it today.

Peace existed for four centuries after the Ligures submitted to the Romans (A.D. 1), and numerous traces of Roman life may be found in the ancient ruins of Eze. The village was captured by the Saracens in 713 and became an important fortified lookout point.

It is apparent that a château must have existed in the eleventh century, for we read that in 1229 such a castle was confiscated by Raimond Beranger. It belonged next to the crown of Anjou-Provence (1246–1388), passed to the House of Savoy (1388–1691), and finally was possessed by Louis XIV, who caused it to be dismantled in 1706. Despite the destruction of the château, the Barony continued under the aegis of the House of Cortina-Turin from 1611 to the Revolution.

An illustrious train of voyagers passed through this typical village of Provence over the centuries. Masséna, Marshal of France, came; then Napoleon in 1811; and finally Pope Pius VII, returning to Rome after his captivity at Fontainebleau.

Despite the royal presence of the Barons, the citizens of Eze Village lived in the simplest manner, enclosed by the massive walls, the fruits of their small terrains, and the work of their hands providing them with all their needs save salt. Their imagination and creativity was expressed only through their religious life, stimulated by the twelve chapels and the oratories which crowded the corners of the village's tiny streets. (One such chapel—"Blessed Cross of the White Penitents"—has been astonishingly restored by the artist Michel-Marie Poulain, a resident of Eze Village.)

Life in Eze Village was materially unchanged from the Middle Ages until 1914, when the establishment of highways, and the installation of electricity and water brought a rebirth to this remote spot which had always been forced by the cruelty of circumstance to live by its fierce motto, "In dying, I am reborn."

Built upon the ruins of ancient châteaux, the Château de la Chèvre d'Or became a restaurant-hotel in 1952. It offers a blend of medieval and provincial styles in its six charming apartments which offer repose to writers, artists, and heads of government. Its terrace and dining room, with a magnificent view reaching to far-off Corsica, accommodate each year a multitude of gourmets who come to sample its famed cuisine.

CHÂTEAU CHOISEUL

Excellent food served in the ancestral home of the Prime Minister to Louis XV.

An ancient twelfth-century home of the Knights of Stainville, this château was one of the most important of the region of Bar. During the Middle Ages, the castle was a powerful fortress complete with towers, ramparts, and a moat. Its majestic staircase has supported the footfalls of royal personages throughout the ages.

From the archives we learn that in 1346 the baronies of Montplanne and Stainville were separated from each other, the Stainville estates being retained by William and Philip de Stainville. These lords considered themselves under the authority of the Dukes of Bar, and at the formation of the seven Collegiate Churches of Lorraine and Bar they constructed, in memory of their father Louis de Stainville and at their own expense, the chapel which still stands across the garden from the present château.

The area frequently has been the scene of wars and desolation. In 1459, the lands of Lavincourt and Stainville are described as being "deserted and abandoned by the calamities of the time and the ravages of the epidemic to such an extent that only three houses are standing upright."

At numerous periods in its history, however, the château has been beautified. The first of these restorations took place in 1634 after a visit of Monsieur de Montalent, governor of Barrois, to Louise, Countess of Stainville. In 1641, oaks were ordered for the reconstruction of the big drawbridge so that all would be in readiness when the Light Cavalry of the Marquis de Pralin arrived to take up garrison in 1642.

Among the illustrious residents of the château we find the name of Count Étienne de Stainville, Colonel of the Regiment of Lorraine, Marshal of the Empire of Austria, and that of his sister, Nicole de Stainville, who married François-Joseph de Choiseul, Baron of Beaupré, thereby giving the château its present name. Their son was named ambassador from the court of France to England and their grandson Étienne François de Choiseul-Stainville (1719–1785) became the noted Prime Minister to Louis XV. In recognition of his excellence, the king elevated Étienne to the Peerage and gave him the royal Château at Amboise.

The handsome crossbar windows on the upper story of the Château Choiseul date from the period of his ministry when Duke Étienne restored, embellished, and decorated his home in French Renaissance style.

The last owner of the fief of Stainville was Thérèse-Felicité, wife of Prince Joseph of Monaco, second son of Honoré III and the ill-fated Princess of Château de Betz. Last victim of the Revolution, the twenty-eight-year-old Princess died on the scaffold on the same fateful day which commemorates the fall of Robespierre.

The château was sold as a national property and possessed by many families until it was purchased (without modern utilities) by Chef and Madame Jung in 1954. They have succeeded in revivifying and modernizing the château without spoiling the unique medieval beauty of its corridors and chambers containing handsome stone fireplaces and heavy, hand-carved oak beams.

Today the culinary genius of Chef Jung attracts all the notables of the international scene to the halls which have preserved to this day the aura of the fabulous Dukes of Lorraine.

CHÂTEAU DE COUDRÉE

A visit among the beauties of Italian Renaissance art.   A perfect place if you're traveling with children.

The Château de Coudrée, facing Lake Léman, had its origin as a sixth-century wooden tower.   Today it contains a wealth of Italian Renaissance decorative art. Its chapel ceiling resembles the Vatican Chapel of the Swiss Guards.   Its Louis XV *boiseries* (wainscoting) still gleam with the polished patina put there long ago. Its Gothic salon with colorful stained-glass windows creates the *ambiance* of medieval serenity and one can enjoy the magnificence of handpainted beams and a polychrome fireplace.

The château was at first a priory for the Abbey of St. Maurice d'Agaune.   It was built on the site where, in the third century, Mauritius, chief of the Theban Legion, became a Christian martyr.

In 1245, the priory was ceded to Beatrix de Greyzier, widow of Henri d'Allinges, whose family beautified the château.   It was a stronghold with massive stone walls replacing earlier light construction and its present form had been established.   It is probable that the mansion was the scene of the Treaty of Sciez, signed in 1289 between Philip of Savoy and Lord de Faucigny, Crown Prince of Vienna.

During long years the stronghold was subjected to successive assaults and sieges.   From 1567 to 1589 profound architectural changes were made to conform to military demands.   These can still be identified as the visitor walks around the château: the large door of the north façade, the adjoining *poterne,* the guard room, the drawbridge, a spiral staircase that replaced ladders that gave access to the dungeon above, the large casement windows, and a second defensive enclosure flanked by four cylindrical towers (uncovered in 1911).   These transformations were scarcely ended when the château was almost entirely burned and dismantled by brigands from Geneva and Bern, leaving us no further trace of its history until the early eighteenth century when a second story was added under the eaves and a large portal was constructed, leading to Lake Léman.   Today this gateway is the main entrance to the château.

Around 1785, the great Italian poet and dramaturgist Count Vittorio Alfieri (a member of the Allinge family) came to the château to conduct his love affair with the Countess d'Albany and to work out the themes for an epic poem and an historic tragedy.

In 1840, the last Marquis Allinge-Coudrée died.   The property passed to his cousins Duc and Ricci, then to the celebrated Italian diplomat, Marquis Cesare Alfieri de Sostegno, and finally to the noted Italian statesman, Baron Cavour. Cavour was not interested in this acquisition and the abandoned château became a farm.   The magnificent tapestries which today adorn the Grand Salon (based on the designs of Rubens and commissioned by Louis XIV as a gift for his Prime Minister, Colbert) were used as curtains for the stables and the ammonia fumes which were present there account for the extraordinary freshness of color which they still possess.

In 1848, Coudrée was inhabited by Monsieur Anatole Bartholoni who aided in the *coup d'état* which made Napoleon III an Emperor.   The property passed to his nephew René Bartholoni, the last private owner of the castle.   This gentleman retained the finest architects and antique dealers to help him restore the château to the grandeur of its Sardinian origins—a grandeur which we still see today at the Château de Coudrée.

CHÂTEAU DE CREISSELS

Family-type meals and comfortable accommodations where glittering personalities of science and art were once welcomed.

Even though the Château de Creissels once belonged to King Henry IV of France, its origin cannot be positively dated. A position of such height must have dominated the valley since earliest antiquity. An act of the year 801 makes mention of Roman objects found in its garden.

In 1272, "Creyssel" was qualified as a viscounty including the baronies of Meyrueis and Roquefeuil united by the marriage of Bernard Anduze to Adelaide de Roquefeuil in 1129.

The name Roquefeuil was derived from the character of the stones found at Creissels, a mixture of white rock (*roche*) and leaves (*feuilles*).

With the marriage of Isabeau Roquefeuil to Hughes, Count of Rodez, the ownership of the château fell to a great family of bishops and archbishops and for nearly a century remained part of the Rodez domains. The archbishop's chamber with its hand-carved woodwork, its matching bed, prayer stool, and piano may be occupied today by guests of the château.

Inherited next by the Armagnac family, it was the home of Jean d'Armagnac, celebrated warrior who rallied the forces of eight hundred French villages under the king to thrust off the yoke of English taxation.

In 1513, Creissels passed to its most illustrious proprietors, the Bourbon.

Life in the château went on without incident. Its daily activities were directed by a series of captains ending with Étienne Rascalon in 1562. In that year Henry de Bourbon became Viscount of Creissels. Shortly thereafter he ascended the throne of France as Henry IV and Creissels was joined to the Crown.

The most significant event in the château's history is its role in the siege of 1628. Assailed by Huguenot forces under the Duke of Rohan, the pitifully outnumbered citizens fought so valiantly that they defeated the adversary before help arrived. Their victory brought Rohan's entire campaign to an end.

Following this event Louis XIII presented Pierre de Crozat de la Croix, captain of the château, with the "ruins, moats, and gardens of the Château de Creyssels."

In 1633 when the king ordered the ramparts demolished only Pierre's home, the present château, was spared.

Repaired with refinement by his son Étienne, the château remained in the De la Croix family until the Revolution when it was sold to the De Gualy family. During the night of September 14, 1814, however, much of the castle's elegance was destroyed according to the family archives. "Two floors fell prey to the flames; all one wing, just built, all the wardrobe, twenty-two beds, table linens, silver, deeds and a considerable library, none of which our position permits us to replace."

In 1936, Madame Marcel Hubin bought Creissels, replenished the library, modernized the facilities, and welcomed to her home the most glittering personalities of science and art. The great opera star, Calvé, was a frequent visitor and her portrait, painted in the costume of Carmen, still hangs in the château.

The story of Creissels ends like a fairy tale, for certainly Madame Hubin must have believed in "Cinderella." She bequeathed her lovely castle to her goddaughter, Madame Austux, who has preserved it intact—proof that sometimes the wishes and dreams of childhood *do* come true.

173

CHÂTEAU DE DIVONNE

A French Spa at its gracious best.

On a terrace looking toward majestic Mont Blanc is perched the Château de Divonne, ancestral home of the Lords of Divonne and Gex. Their coat-of-arms remains the insignia of the community of Divonne-les-Bains, famous spa of the French Alps.

We know that this château was in existence earlier than 1195 and that Étienne de Divonne founded the Abbey of Bonmont here in 1124.

Two hundred years later, by the treaty of 1355, the Lords of Divonne became the vassals of the Counts of Savoy, but they continued to inhabit their castle, enlarging it considerably with the passing years. In 1536, the Lords of Divonne were overcome by armies from Bern and Geneva and in 1589, the château was burned and dismantled.

In an inventory taken for Albert-Eugène de la Forest-Divonne much later on, the château is represented as having "quite mediocre dimensions; about a dozen rooms, the cabinet of the Grotto, the Salon of the Ladies, the wing of the 'sleeper.'" The contradiction is apparent. Numerous parts of the château were in such bad state of repair that they were not even described. In an extensive restoration the château was surrounded by a high wall with twelve towers, the emplacements of which are still in the park of the present château.

A chapel certainly existed in the ancient château, but it had disappeared by 1714. It is obvious from an inscription on the bell of the parish church that the lords attended Mass there. The engraving testifies that the patrons were "high and mighty Master Lord Sir Claude de la Forest-Divonne, Colonel of the Grenadiers of France and high and mighty Madame Mary de la Rivoire, his wife."

Apparently such an arrangement was unsuitable to Albert-Eugène and between 1730 and 1735 he constructed the "Chapel of the Annunciation," which stands to the right of the château. Inside are handsome polychrome murals. In its subterrane lie the remains of the family members of Forest-Divonne. A black marble plaque enumerates in letters of gold all of their names starting with Albert-Eugène.

From 1765 to 1770 Claude de la Forest-Divonne remodeled the château in the style of Louis XV.

The château was badly mistreated during the Revolution, when the archives and family portraits were burned. Several family portraits, still bearing the slashes of the Republicans' swords, are hanging in the corridors of the castle. In 1850, Louis Marie François de la Forest-Divonne transformed the castle once again, placing the remains of the Louis XV structure between two heavy wings of new construction. With the lack of taste which marked this period in history he had the twelve magnificent towers razed. A delegation of citizens of Divonne requested that he spare some remembrance of the past and he agreed to preserve the ancient twelfth-century *poterne* of the château with its eight-foot-thick walls. It is to be found a short distance from the terrace of the château, to the right of the great arched portal of the sixteenth-century edifice which endures, too sturdy to have been thrown down by the forces of nature or man.

These antique remnants, rising stark in the flowered entry, remind us once more that the thread of an historic past is all around us in the gay holiday atmosphere of the Château de Divonne.

175

CHÂTEAU FÈRE-EN-TARDENOIS

Playground of King François I and his comrade, Commander-in-Chief of the Armies, Anne de Montmorency.

Fère-en-Tardenois was constructed between 1206 and 1260 as a fortified castle by Robert de Dreux, grandson of Louis VI, King of France. Little is known of it save that it belonged to the royal family Valois-Orléans-Angoulême from 1328 to 1528 when it was given by Louise of Savoy, mother of François I, to Anne de Montmorency, Governor General of France and Chancellor to six kings from Louis XII to Charles IX. A warrior, diplomat, minister, devotee of the arts, Montmorency was the most powerful man in all France next to the king. He was in possession of six hundred feudal properties, one hundred thirty châteaux and baronies, four mansions in Paris and numerous other holdings. Through his five sons and seven daughters, all married into the highest families of the land, he was able to keep his finger on the nation's pulse. Builder of exquisite châteaux at Chantilly and Ecouen, he undertook to create at Fère-en-Tardenois a country seat of relaxation. He ordered the monumental bridge that still stands in the garden of the château to be thrust across the moat.

The bridge is said to have been designed by the famous Jean Bullant (Musée Carnavalet), architect of the homes and tombs of Henry II and Catherine de Médicis. It rests on five huge full-curved arches supported by rectangular pilings. A double gallery, the second story of which is partly demolished, rises above. The embellishments of the gallery and portico are attributed to Jean Goujon, sculptor and architect noted for his bas-reliefs and his decoration of the Louvre Museum.

Crossing this beautiful bridge one reaches the ruins of eight huge towers. At the base of these towers are beds of stones arranged like the teeth of a saw, an architectural peculiarity of which there is no other existing example.

The château passed to the son of the great *Connetable* Montmorency and then to his grandson Henry II, whose plot to overthrow Richelieu cost his head at Toulouse in 1632, as well as the confiscation of Fère-en-Tardenois.

Louis XIII returned the castle to Henry's daughter, Charlotte Montmorency. (Henry IV had once so passionately loved her that he almost fought the King of Spain to retrieve her when, on her wedding night, she fled to Belgium with her husband, Prince of Condé, in order to avoid the king's advances.)

The castle finally was inherited by Philip Egalité. So anxious was he for the approval of the Republicans that he ordered his own château at Fère partially demolished. The defacement of the Valois-Orléans-Angoulême and Montmorency crests on the entrance of the bridge was perpetrated with his permission, but the inaccessibility of those same coats-of-arms on the pillars below makes it possible for us to appreciate their handsome imprint today.

To further his political ambitions, Philip sold the furnishings and fixtures of the castle. Those which remained were taken to public auction by his creditors in 1793.

Thus ended the glorious era of Fère-en-Tardenois, pleasure palace of kings.

In 1863 the present château, once a wing of the Royal castle, was restored. Converted to a hotel in 1956, it offers a wealth of gastronomic specialties.

CHÂTEAU DE LÉVEZOU

*The rooms are small, but the food is excellent here in the former
residence of the Bishops of Rodez.*

Salles-Curan, the location of the Château de Lévezou, was an important place
in the Gallo-Roman period when it was identified as a famous highway called
"Lou Camy Farrat."

As far back as historians can trace, the township was owned by the Counts
of Rodez (also Viscounts of Creissels). A stone encased in the wall of the church
bears the family coat of arms.

In 1270, Salles-Curan belonged to Vivian, Bishop of Rodez who retreated to
the château to deliver himself from the numerous murderers, brigands, extortion-
ists, and incendiaries to whom he frequently fell prey.

Through the decades the château, located next to the Church of Notre Dame,
continued to be the fortified summer palace of the Bishops of Rodez, but at the
end of the Hundred Years' War the great dangers seemed to be over. In the new
climate of peace the lords wished to leave their fortresses and construct more
agreeable types of châteaux. One of those nobles who wished to live in a more
gracious atmosphere was Bishop Guillaume de La Tour. Tiring of a stultified
existence behind walls he preferred the liberty of access and exit enjoyed by
secular Lords. He arranged with the citizens of Salles-Curan that a new château
be built for him, at the cost of the community, near the tower of the Portal of St.
Geraud (presently the actual tower of the Château de Lévezou). The new château
became the property of the Bishop de La Tour. In return he declared "unfeudal"
some of the lands around his old castle which were parceled and given to the
townspeople for the building of small homes. The rear walls of these domiciles
were supported by the ramparts of the old château. In addition the citizens were
permitted to buy from the Bishop twenty parcels of the surrounding terrain. Thus
in the fifteenth century the desire of Bishop de La Tour to live free of the walls
which reminded him of war led him to create the first formula for land reform
carried out by a democratic method of exchange between a nobleman and his
community.

The price and details of construction for this new château was given by P.
Combettes, master mason at St. Beauzely in 1442, at "130 moutons d'or" plus a
house for Monsieur Combettes. Today the door to the château courtyard, built
by M. Combettes is classified by the Beaux Arts. It may be observed to the left
of the château's entrance.

The new Château de Lévezou, just as the old, served as a summer residence
of the Bishops of Rodez. Abandoned a long time before the Revolution, it was
sold during the Terror as a national property. The history of its tenancy is lost
until it was purchased as a residence in 1910 by the grandfather of its present
owner, Monsieur Bouviala, whose mother converted the castle into a commercial
enterprise under the title of "Auberge de Campagne."

Now, after four years as a Master Chef in Paris, Monsieur Bouviala has returned to his birthplace to assume the restoration of the château. The first steps
have been taken. The ancient kitchen has been changed into a handsome dining
room and café where today's visitors sample gastronomic specialties prepared in
the ancient fireplace according to the age-old traditions of French cuisine.

CHÂTEAU DE LA MALÈNE
ET MONTESQUIOU

The site where the Barons of Montesquiou planned the brilliant
strategies for which they are reknowned.

At the center of the Tarn Canyon entering the village of La Malène the eye is struck by the sight of a pretty château ornamented by a central tower and two small towers with mullioned windows.

In the middle of the principal façade there is a remarkable entry of the sixteenth century and a terrace shaded by venerable chestnut trees which gives a view of the limpid Tarn River.

To the left of the château courtyard there is a large door surmounted by a double crest and an arcade of eight mullioned windows which have been restored. On the right is the seventeenth-century wing which makes one wonder what secrets are locked in this once proud stronghold of the valiant de Montesquiou.

A place of passage since earliest antiquity, La Malène has been invaded many times.

In the fourth century St. Ilère established a vast monastery on the heights. To quell the restless Lozerians he had to call for the aid of Thierry, son of King Clovis.

Three hundred years later this monastery, "Castrum de La Malène," nicknamed Castel Merlet, suffered its most terrible pillaging and looting at the hands of the vengeful Saracens returning south after their disastrous defeat at Poitiers in 732.

The château of today stands at the apex of a property which contained four castles, all of which were inhabited by the de Montesquiou for a period of 1500 years without interruption.

Vestiges of the first château are on the emplacement of the Castel Merlet. They form the foundation of the existing château.

The second château was established directly opposite the first on the rock called "Ron de Montesquiou" which may still be seen across the street from the present château.

At the end of the property bordering the Tarn there stood the famous Château du Plagnol (thirteenth century), stakeout point of the Catholics during the Religious Wars. Taken in battle time and again by the Marquis d'Albignac and the Duke of Rohan, it was finally reconquered by Pierre de Montesquiou, Marshal of France. In the ruins there are still traces of a red cannon ball hurled from the promontory above in the final conflict.

The Montesquiou finally established themselves in the present Château de La Malène in which, during the Revolution, a bloody page of history was written.

Numerous Royalists had taken refuge in the castle with its prodigious natural defenses of rock. When the Revolutionaries attacked in large numbers, some Royalists were able to escape through the underground passages which the Montesquiou had built to connect their four châteaux. In reprisal, the Republicans burned La Malène rounding up all the remaining inhabitants in the château's court of honor. Twenty-one men were taken to the guillotine at Florac while twenty-five others were imprisoned at Rodez to be executed later. Madame de Montesquiou herself was forced to hide away in one of the grottos where she became blind.

Emerging after the Revolution she courageously rebuilt the present château which, by successive marriages, was inherited through the female line by de Montesquiou until 1957 when it was converted to the historical hotel of today.

CHÂTEAU DE MERCUÈS

*A dominating view of the Lot Valley from the palace
of the Archbishops of Cahors.*

A few miles from Cahors in the valley of the Lot the land suddenly rises to reveal the breath-taking vision of the Château de Mercuès. From its green pinnacle it dominates a view of the ramparts of Cahors, the high steeples of the Cathedral, and the famous towers of Pont Valentré, most beautiful fortified bridge in all France.

First the site of a Gallo-Roman camp called "Castrum Mercurii," then a Temple consecrated to Mercury, the intermediate history of the place is obscured until the eleventh century when we know it was a stronghold. Later it was the focal point of amusing events.

When Charles VII came to the throne in 1422, Le Quercy was one of the few provinces remaining under the French Crown. However, Mercuès was an English fortification. Finding the presence of the English intolerable, a company of Quercynois laid siege to the castle in 1428. Captain de Buch was sent with 1500 Englishmen to relieve the garrison, but he changed his mind about fighting when he saw the fierce determination of his adversaries. Deciding to negotiate, he permitted the Quercynois to buy back their own castle for the price of 1600 sheep (24 sous) and a piece of damask.

During the sixteenth century Mercuès passed into the possession of the Bishops of Cahors. It served them as a palace for three hundred years during which time, except for brief periods of violence, many beautiful transformations were made—notably the building of the terrace carried on under the aegis of Bishop Habert, from 1627 to 1636, who called the men of Cahors to the palace in order to isolate them from a raging epidemic and to provide them with work and food. The skillful fashioning of the balustrade makes the terrace of Mercuès one of the finest of its kind.

Some years later Bishops Henri Guillaume Le Jay and Henri de Briqueville de la Luzerne added the massive western part of the castle which is typical of the period of Louis XIV.

Perhaps because the peasant revolutionaries remembered that many of the Bishops had been beneficent and generous, Mercuès was spared in the Terror of 1789. Sold as national property, it passed from hand to hand, sometimes belonging to the Bishops and sometimes to secular proprietors.

The excellent state of preservation which Mercuès enjoys today is largely due to Monsignor Grimardias, one of its last Bishop owners, who at great personal cost restored the two main towers to their full height in his passion to see the castle as imposing as it was in the days of its greatest splendor.

In 1905, after the separation of Church and State, Mercuès reverted to the government. Its furnishings, tapestries, and portraits were removed to the sacristy of the Cahors Cathedral, where they are still on display.

From 1905–1914 Mercuès was open to the public, but in 1914 it was purchased by Dr. J. L. Fauré, professor of medicine and surgery, who turned it into a gracious country home. On his death in 1944, his daughters, Mesdames Denise Labusquière and Adrienne Jalaquier converted the castle to a hotel, maintaining the dignified serenity of their home—the palace and gardens once so soothing to the spirits of the Archbishops of Cahors.

CHÂTEAU DE MEYRARGUES

Ancient stronghold of the mightiest Lords of Provence.

Meyrargues, village of less than a thousand souls, contains one of the oldest fortified sites of France classified by the Beaux Arts.

The location is mentioned by Greek historians as being a Celtic outpost as early as 600 B.C.

In 122 B.C., finding the water at Aix insufficient, the Romans built the Aqueduct of Traconnade, of which two complete arches and one single column remain in the olive groves below the Château de Meyrargues.

Marius, the Roman, established a camp on this site called "Marii-Agger," from which the castle's name was derived. The funeral tablet of Septimus Flaccus embedded in the left wall of the château's entry is a vestige of the period.

The first château was built by Pons Le Majeur, the east façade being constructed with stones left from the demolition of the aqueduct. In 970 when Count William I partitioned the lands of Provence, Hughes Les Baux became second Lord of Meyrargues and the history of the castle seems without incident until 1140 when the château was ravaged by the conflicts of Raimond Les Baux and Raimond Berenger, Count of Barcelona, in their greed for title of Count of Provence. (Paradoxically, during this period the beautiful Abbey of Silvacane was founded by Raimond Les Baux and the Chapel of St. Christopher was added to the château.)

The next years were full of strife. In 1304 Hughes Les Baux (Tenth Lord) was forced to turn Meyrargues over to King Charles II to satisfy his creditors.

The château became the property of the Counts of Provence. Its prestige increased until the turbulence and misdeeds of Raimond, Viscount of Turenne, brought a scourge on all the territory. In siege after siege the majestic Meyrargues was desecrated. Pillaged, sacked, and burned, it reverted to the king who later returned it to Antoinette of Turenne and her husband, Boucicaut. The magnificent repairs made by them are responsible for the major appearance of the château today.

In 1442, King René "in recognition of service and loyalty" presented Meyrargues to Arteluche d'Allagonia. Times of peace and alliances of marriage enhanced its fortunes until the holocaust of the Religious Wars. Some years later Meyrargues again was confiscated——this time by Henry IV.

1623 marks the significant legal actions which gave the inhabitants of Meyrargues the rights and privileges of co-operative government and set the stage for self-government almost one hundred seventy years before the Revolution.

In 1625, Meyrargues became the holding of the benevolent Leon de Valbelle. His power-mad brother, Provost of Marseilles, stirred such hatred in the Governor of Provence that the château was attacked and only the outer structure remained.

The innocent Baron Leon was forced to repair the château completely. His son François continued the beautification and his grandson, Cosmo, added all the handsome elements which create its powerful aspect today.

So fair were the Valbelle in their dealings with the community that their holdings were protected by the citizenry during the Revolution and the castle with all its furnishings remained in the possession of Albine Caussigny-Valbelle until her death in 1851.

Abandoned for a century, the great château was rescued from ruin and converted to a hotel in 1952. Today, with its reputation for excellent cuisinè it continues to dominate the valley of the Durance just as it did when it was the stronghold of the mightiest Lords of Provence.

CHÂTEAU DE MIMONT

A rare opportunity to live en famille *surrounded by exquisite antiques.*

"Au bois comme à table . . ." In the woods as though at the table . . . is the motto of Château de Mimont.

The great woods that surround this castle encourage the Chasse à Courre, the practice of hunting on horseback with the aid of hounds such wild animals as stag or wild boar. Today this sport is an exciting way to procure savory, wholesome meat, but before the Middle Ages, it was an essential method of destroying the beasts which endangered crops and preyed on the lives of the citizenry.

The venerated traditions of the chase were established in the twelfth century and were further developed from the medieval times up to the Revolution. The lavishness of the riding costumes, the science of the hunt, the creation of the broad range of fanfares, the finesse in the breeding and development of fine strains of horses and dogs, the growth of a special vocabulary, the improvement of the techniques of horsemanship, all took place during these centuries and have been perpetuated by the lovers of this pastime to the present.

This sport is practiced according to the ancient traditions at Mimont from November to March. Today, the colorful pageant of horses, dogs, men, and animals locked in a life and death struggle is re-enacted at the château exactly as it has been performed in France for fifteen centuries.

Before the Roman conquest, the site of Mimont was the last defense of the Morvan region. Some fifty miles from Paris, on the route to Vichy and the Mediterranean, Mimont dominated the Valley of the Loire. Ruins in the beautiful woods that surround the park seem to indicate that Mimont has a much more mysterious ancient history. There remain on the property some Dolmen—large flat stones laid across upright stone supports—which archaeologists believe are prehistoric Druid tombs or monuments. A grotto and some stones of sacrifice seem to give further evidence that Mimont was a place of predilection of these ancient Celtic soothsayers and priests.

In the eleventh century an Abbey existed at Mimont, but only a small stone statue of a monk and some vestiges of the emplacement of a wall remain from that period. The Abbey was destroyed during the Revolution and at the beginning of the nineteenth century the present château was constructed on its foundation.

It is believed that Mimont served as a resting spot for Emperor Napoleon III during his visits at Vichy. It came into the possession of its current owner, the Alasnier family, after the World War and was transformed into a château-hotel in 1962. The furnishings of the castle are entirely composed of authentic antiques of the eighteenth and nineteenth centuries. There is a remarkable suite of Charles X living-room furnishings as well as floors of Louis XIV parquet, a pink marble staircase, ancient tapestries, oriental carpets, original paintings, and Regency chandeliers of bronze gilt from which are appended crystals by Baccarat.

These artifacts of the past adorn every corner of the château and surround the traveler with a unique atmosphere of tradition and "grand classe."

CHÂTEAU DE MONTREUIL

Modern comfort on the property of the Citadel, ancient fortress known as the "Sentinel of the Northern Frontier."

The actual Château de Montreuil was built after World War II on the property of the ancient Citadel, where one may visit the historical ramparts and vestiges of the mighty fortress itself. Even though the *Relais* is of our time, the surroundings are of important historical significance.

In the past Montreuil has been a religious center, a commanding fortress, and a prosperous commercial community. Today it is only a rendezvous for painters who are seduced by its old streets, its ramparts, and its natural beauties as they must have appeared to the searching eyes of St. Saulve when he established his monastery twelve centuries ago.

In the centuries following the population grouped itself about the monastery walls for protection against the northern invaders, but a town was not actually formed until near the end of the ninth century when Hilgold I, Monk of Riquier, built a fortified château, the chapel of St. Firmin, and four churches.

Montreuil soon became the "Town of Monasteries" and moreover, the home of the Church of St. Saulve where the remains of almost all the Saints of Brittany repose. The city became a place of pilgrimage for the faithful who flocked to venerate the sainted relics and treasures.

Caught in the tides of wars and invasions, Montreuil was united to the Crown by Hugh Capet in 987. To avoid further trouble, he built a powerful fortified château on the site of the present Citadel, especially interesting to us because it dates the property on which the Château de Montreuil stands. Part of this ancient fortress endures. It is known as the Tower of Queen Berthe where in 1091, Philip I imprisoned his wife, so that he might seduce and marry Bertrade, wife of the Duke of Anjou. Years later King Louis VI retrieved the body of his mother to place it in the sepulcher of St. Denis.

In the mid-fifteenth century an earthquake destroyed six of the town's most beautiful churches and subsequent repairs reduced the dimensions of these edifices and lessened their opulence.

The almost forty thousand inhabitants of fifteenth-century Montreuil enjoyed great prosperity. Cloth industries flourished, religious structures abounded, the reknowned Carmelite liqueurs were developed, and ships came right to the foot of the Citadel for trading. Montreuil's fortifications were also kept in good repair and a complete reconstruction made in 1517 by François I can still be perceived. Montreuil's fortunes turned with the siege of 1537 and the pestilence of 1596 which killed three-fifths of the citizenry. Montreuil never regained its prominence after these catastrophes, though Henry IV ordered additional fortifications to augment those already surrounding the Citadel. Louis XIII ordered them further arranged and in 1689, the great architect, Vauban, enlarged and strengthened them. They were used as general headquarters for the left wing of Napoleon's Army, were employed as British General Headquarters in World War I when the Tower of Queen Berthe was an allied telephone and telegraph post, and were used again for the same purpose in World War II.

Today the visitor to the Château de Montreuil may walk across the garden to visit these historical ruins of the fortress which once made this quiet village reknowned as the "Sentinel of the Northern Frontier."

LA PETITE AUBERGE
DE NOVES

Fabulous Food served on a high hill overlooking the
Papal Palace at Avignon.

The property of La Petite Auberge, originally known as Le Devès, was under the immediate temporal and spiritual authority of the Bishops of Avignon for many centuries until 1400 when its agricultural value declined to such a degree that the Bishop ceded the lands to wealthy friends in the Duchy. For two hundred years it passed through the hands of several nobles and clerics and in 1605, Bishop Bordini sold the land to Denis Roux, a captain of the Catholic forces. The first buildings of Le Devès, now La Petite Auberge itself, appear to date from that period. The château is described in historical documents of the time as having had battlements, a stable, and a dovecot. It passed quickly into the possession of the Faculty of Law Professors from Avignon, then in 1614, to a Monsieur Gouze; and in 1632, to a Monsieur De Tacke.

In the first years of the eighteenth century the members of the Senchon family, living at Noves, grew rich in agriculture and elevated themselves into accounting and finally into the law. In 1718, Francis Senchon bought the part of the property called "Bournissac" and in 1727, his son, Baudile Senchon de Bournissac, bought the adjoining portion of "Le Devès."

Baudile's son Étienne was guillotined during the Revolution for participating in the siege of Lyons against the Republicans. As a consequence, when peace was reestablished it was Étienne's three sons, former officers of the king's forces, who took over the large family home at Noves. They busied themselves with farming and took part in the religious quarrels of the era. Refusing to adhere to the "Concordat of Napoleon," they remained faithful to their Bishops, around whom they formed a group called "The Little Church." Le Devès became a religious retreat. The brothers enlarged the château by constructing the actual west wing of La Petite Auberge and in 1833, an east wing was built and edified as a vast chapel in which the three brothers de Bournissac wished to be entombed. Their remains rested there until 1950, when removal to the church grounds was deemed advisable in view of the new destiny reserved for this ancient property.

In that year Le Devès became the possession of its current proprietors, Monsieur and Madame Lalleman, who had planned to retire there from their busy life in Paris. Finding inactivity unsuitable, they renamed the mansion "La Petite Auberge" and transformed it into the elegant restaurant-hotel we see today, high on its ancient hill overlooking the winding Durance River and the distant outline of the Papal Palace at Avignon.

CHÂTEAU DE PILATE
ET FONTAGER

One of the most historically and archeologically interesting
châteaux along the road.

It is certain that the Château de Pilate et Fontager is one of the oldest in France. As recently as 1963, workers enlarging its terrace suddenly struck their tools on some resistant objects. Believing them at first to be stones couched in the soil, they continued their work until the stroke of the pick turned up some red bricks and part of a human skeleton in perfect condition. Work was immediately suspended in the suspicion that the discovery might be significant. On the following day, supervised by archeologists, the workers uncovered ten more such beautifully preserved skeletons. The irregularities of the ground indicated the presence of about eighty more such tombs, all constructed with flat tiles.

The detection of this cemetery imbedded under a courtyard where people had been circulating for centuries, might have been expected, since mosaics from the Gallo-Roman period were exposed in the protecting wall of this same château in 1817.

It is thought that perhaps these ruins mark the emplacement of Pontius Pilate's habitation. On maps of the Dauphiné made in the sixteenth and seventeenth centuries, these buildings are called "Château de Pilate." Banished in disgrace after the events in Judea, Pilate was made governor of Vienne in 37 and is said to have killed himself in 39 by jumping from a tower of the château. Certainly the village of "Ponsas" takes its name from the words Pontius Pilate.

The opinion of many of the archeologists who have come to observe the findings made at the château is that the sarcophagi and their contents date from the era of Constantine in the third century. The skeletons seem to be those of warriors or of members of a large family inhabiting the château during that epoch. No description has yet been given to the bricks and crushed tiles of the sepulchers, but the skeletons are for the most part perfectly preserved in the sand and clay.

The presence of implements and vases inside the coffins substantiates the theory that these dead belonged to Roman and pagan families, since it was customary in that period for the living to carry food to the dead.

During Middle Ages the château at Fontager was a stronghold of the Count de Vals. Later, in the fourteenth century, the illustrious Du Bugey family remodeled their fortified house into a gentleman's manor. (The excavations of the terrace have also uncovered the remains of Madame De Gruel, owner of the château in 1596, buried with her baby in her arms, both apparent victims of cholera but certainly these remains have nothing to do with those of the era of Constantine). Different parts of the château display the coats of arms of the De Chastelard, De Vernoux, Flotte de Roquevaire, De Boissieu and De Croze. It was Madame De Croze who originally turned the castle into a hotel in 1925.

Today the château is being restored to its former stature. Every luxury is present and a small museum to house the "finds" of the archeologists is being established to remind us that perhaps the earth of the château has not yet given up all its secrets.

HOSTELLERIE DE LA POSTE

Time-honored stopover of Emperor Napoleon on his triumphant return from the Isle of Elba.

The origins of Hostellerie de la Poste, world-famous restaurant-hotel, are described by its owner Mr. René Hure in his short essay on the development of French hotelery.

If we had the dubious job of writing a general history of our hotelery we can find its source in the beginnings of our roadways and our methods of travel which gave it life.

In France it is useful to realize the worth, after the fifteenth century, of the routes of communication judiciously set up by the Romans at the four cardinal points of legendary Gaul.

Civilization lending a helping hand, these ribbon-like roadways used by the early isolated travelers were quickly marked out by the utilitarian vehicles taking advantage of public transportation.

It is thus near 1575, in the last years of the reign of Charles IX, that France saw its routes adorned with horse-drawn conveyances. ("It is a clean vessel, for holding several persons, suspended on a carriage of four wheels, pulled by six strong percherons; a convenient vehicle," adds the Trévoux Dictionary, "to use to go to the city and to the country.")

During almost four centuries our vital lines of access, from north to south, from southwest to east, came to know an ever-growing prosperity, thanks to the horse-drawn carriage and all its consequences! But from the post chaise of the Great Century to the romantic "diligence," in voyaging via the stage coach or the traveling "berline," all these turn-outs had to provide, all along the way, propitious posting houses to change the team, to check the steadfastness of the carriage and above all to provide opportunity for the travelers to rest and restore themselves fully.

Thus was born in the seventeenth century our national hotel industry, thanks to the pleasant, well-placed inns and to the good halting places on the important routes where the tourist found at the sight of the insignia (painted on a sheet-metal plaque, grating its rusty hinges in every wind) the comfort of a good lodging and the bliss of good cuisine.

Founded in 1707, the Hostellerie de la Poste at Avallon is an ancient stage-coach stop on the route from Switzerland to the Côte d'Azur. Many illustrious visitors have enjoyed its facilities. Frederick William, king of Prussia, the Duke of Orleans, future king of France, also visited and in 1815, Emperor Napoleon made a triumphal stop on his passage back from Elba.

In our time it has become a halt of grand class. Its interior garden has welcomed the Sultans of Morocco, and the Duke and Duchess of Windsor. In 1944, while the hotel was being repaired after World War II, General Eisenhower was discovered taking pictures in the courtyard. As a young bachelor, President John F. Kennedy occupied the "Chambre de Napoléon."

Hostellerie de la Poste, its gastronomic reputation reaching the four corners of the earth, is the departure point for trips throughout Burgundy and into the Morvan, a region rich in châteaux, abbeys, museums, fortified towns, and beautiful lakes.

In its famous cellar repose four hundred wines and numerous whiskies and liqueurs under the supervision of Monsieur Charles Colin, the world's most authoritative Sommelier.

Cloaked in the luxury of modern times, the Hostellerie de la Poste offers the traveler the welcome of former centuries and one of the best cuisines in all of France.

CHÂTEAU DE PRANGEY

Trysting place of royal lovers.

The Château de Prangey lies in the heart of Burgundy. Its first Lords are mentioned in 1211 and, in 1315, the Duke of Burgundy made an award to Guy, Lord of Prangey, the last truly of that name to which any historic allusion is made. However, the place is associated with very beguiling events, for during this epoch Marguerite of Burgundy, Queen of Navarre, and her sisters-in-law, Blanche de la Marche, and Jeanne de Poitiers, were accused of adultery and apprehended. The inquest proclaimed Jeanne innocent but Marguerite and Blanche were convicted of having had as lovers two officers of their court, Phillip and Gauthier d'Aulnay. Put to torture, these knights swore to having committed the crime of adultry, "during three years and in the most inviolable places." They were condemned to atrocious corporal punishment. The princesses were imprisoned.

It is firmly believed that the Château de Prangey was the scene of the clandestine amours of Marguerite of Navarre. Some time after the trial Louis le Hutin, her husband, desirous of marrying his cousin Clementine of Hungary, rid himself of his wife by having her smothered as she lay in her prison.

"The Legend of the Tower of Nesle" by Alexander Dumas, Père, makes of Queen Marguerite some sort of strumpet, a rather unfair interpretation in view of the circumstances of her demise.

In the years that followed the château passed through the hands of the Baudoncourt family, the de Saulx family, and the magistrates of Dijon. In the sixteenth century it was repurchased by Field Marshal de Saulx-Tavannes.

The constant passage of the French and foreign armies across the Haute-Marne during the reign of Louis XIII was catastrophic. We read a report in the town register by the Curé of the period, Jean Connefort:

> In the month of August 1636 there arrived in the land (Prangey) the enemy army of Gallas and that of the king, commanded by Monsieur le Cardinal de la Valette, (Louis de Nogaret of Château d'Ayres) . . . the quarters of the king were made at Prangey which was entirely pillaged and ruined without there being anything left, which brought sickness to Prangey that died there . . . more than 1200 persons . . . All were buried . . . by me, called Curé of the place, and one Vicar.

Despite the holocaust the château was purchased by the Pietrequin family which remained until the Revolution. Philibert Pietriquin, Knight of the Council of Langres, took the title of Lord of Prangey and restored the principal building, attaching handsome galleries to the towers protecting the entry. At the same time the celebrated André Le Nôtre, Director of the Royal Gardens of Louis XIV, redesigned the park and made his first plantings of Italian poplars. The garden still carries his distinctive imprint.

The château's history from the Terror until 1910 is obscured. Then, the château was purchased by the Billebaud family. Prangey served as their private home until 1945, when the first paying guests were received. With the addition of modern conveniences and fine cuisine the château still offers the privilege of that same remoteness which once made the castle an ideal trysting place for royal lovers.

CHÂTEAU DE PRAY

A former shelter of gentlemen and ladies attached to the Royal Court of Amboise.

At some steps from the Royal Château of Amboise stands a small castle . . . the Château de Pray, birthplace of the Association of Châteaux-Hotels de France. Its beauties remain unspoiled by the vicissitudes of the feudal epoch, the whims of royalty, or the intricate material changes of the modern world.

This lordly house offers an imposing view of the Loire. Its military aspect, established during the time of its first proprietor Herardus, Archbishop of Tours in 865, is happily blended with the more comfortable elements found in the royal homes of the seventeenth-century classical period.

The château has sheltered numerous families attached to the service of the king. The short distance separating it from the Royal Château made it a perfect stopover for royal horseback-riding excursions and during that period it was used as a hunting lodge, a setting for political plots, or a rendezvous for lovers.

In the reign of Charles VIII, who was born at Amboise, a great taste for luxury developed. Furnishings were opulent. Tapestries, sumptuous accouterments to dining, armor rooms, aviaries, libraries, all had to be supervised, maintained, packed, and unpacked. Under François I scientists, poets, and artists flocked to the court. Women became an integral part of court life for the first time. Homes had to be found for these multitudes. One such is the famous Château de Clos Lucé, final residence of Leonardo da Vinci, who died there in 1519. It stands only one mile from the Château de Pray.

From 1330, the families living at Château de Pray were directly connected to the court at Amboise: the Captain of the Guard, Officers of the "Louveterie" (masters of the wolf hunt), Managers of the Cooking Implements, Confidantes and Ladies-in-Waiting, High Chamberlains in charge of the king's living quarters, Chiefs of Ammunition, etc. From the time of François I about 15,000 people constantly surrounded the king. Henry III was known to have had 200 gentlemen-in-waiting and more than 1000 archers, in addition to the nobelmen and their "households" in residence at the Royal Castle or at castles nearby, such as the Château de Pray.

After the bloody suppression of a Protestant plot at Amboise in 1560, the Kings abandoned the Royal Château and thus the Château de Pray was also abandoned. The entire Loire Valley fell into a commercial decline.

At the beginning of the eighteenth century Louis XV presented the Château d'Amboise to the Duc de Choiseul, of whom we read in the history of the Château Choiseul. The presence of this great Minister of Foreign Affairs, who repaired the misfortunes of the Seven Years' War and who was responsible for the French acquisition of Corsica, cast the last glow of glory on Amboise and on neighboring Château de Pray.

Confiscated during the Revolution the Château de Pray has since been occupied by families outside the main stream of history but nevertheless worthy of merit for having preserved its handsome stained-glass windows, its terrace overlooking the Loire, its massive towers with their winding staircases, and its beautiful wood paneling. All these elements add to the picture of residential elegance and countrylike charm which prevails today at Château de Pray.

HOSTELLERIE DU PRIEURÉ

The exquisite view of the Loire heightens the dining pleasure and the joy of repose.

In the sixth century Gregory de Tours, Bishop, theologian, and historian, wrote of the Prieuré as one of the high places in the region of Saumur. This height, dominating the Loire, was a fortified camp called "Orvanne" or "Orval" by the Gallo-Romans. It was situated about four hundred feet away from the present park of the château. Its disappearance seems to have coincided with an uprising of the peasants of Gaul called "The Revolt of the Bagaudes" and with the numerous Norman invasions which ravaged the banks of the Loire.

At the border of the park of the Prieuré stands a cemetery where, during the last few years, such ruins of archaeological significance as stone sarcophagi, and nests of ancient shells on many levels of ground have been found. Several of the graves give evidence of primitive cremation and pagan and Christian inhumation, proving that it was in use over a considerable number of centuries. It is incontestable that this ancient necropolis dates at least from the Gallo-Roman times and that the property of the Prieuré is of like age.

After the expulsion of the Normans in the tenth century there is indication that ancient stones of "La Cité" were used in the construction of St. Peter's Church in Saumur by the Benedictine Monks of St. Florent de Saumur, who also used the stones in the building of their Prieuré at Chênehutte.

In the fifteenth century a restoration and enlargement to the Prieuré was initiated which continued into the sixteenth century. Elements of the old walls rebuilt at that time are to be found in the present structure—gables, a door with accolade surmounted by a coat of arms, a hexagonal tower surrounding a vast circular staircase of stone, the gallery, the large fireplaces adorned with leaves and crouching animals, and attic eaves with broad beams of rough-hewn wood.

The priests fled during the Revolution and the church was battered. Only some debris remained near the cemetery which was subsequently grouped with the remains of the ancient Prieuré for the building of a manor house, the basis of the present château.

In the beginning of the nineteenth century the Prieuré was restored by its owners, the Counts of Laubespan and Castellane, in the Renaissance character one actually sees now. The structure was surrounded with the vast terraces which still offer a view of the Loire Valley, Tours, and even Angers—a panorama speared by the heights of the famous historic châteaux of Langeais, Bourgueil, Port Bouley, Launay, Saumur, Boumois, Beaufort, and Angers. Burned by the Germans in 1944, the rehabilitation of Prieuré has included a vast new dining salon which allows the eye to trace the route of the monks as they made their three mile walk each day to the Church of St. Peter from Chênehutte-les-Tuffeaux along the bank of the Loire, past the Château de Saumur whose terraces are draped in woods jeweled with the white and glowing rocks from which the region gets its name. Below one sees the ribbon of the river. The ensemble forms a lasting impression of the true color and unique beauty which are always associated with the Valley of the Loire and with the view from the heights of the Prieuré.

LE PRIEURÉ

Charm and comfort in the priory and gardens of a Cardinal's palace.

Avignon is one of the most beautiful sights of the Rhône Valley. Surrounded by ramparts, the city is dominated by its Cathedral and by the colossal outline of the Palace of the Popes.

Across the Rhône other towers pierce the sky: the tower of King Philippe Le Bel and the remains of Fort St. Andre (two symbols of royal power in the face of church domination). At the foot of these bastions of the Middle Ages extends Villeneuve-les-Avignon, home of Le Prieuré.

At the beginning of the fourteenth century factional disputes had made residence in Rome impossible for the Popes. At the insistence of Philippe Le Bel (who thought to make the Pope an instrument of his own will), Clement V installed himself in France in a small country estate. But his successor, Jean XXII (1245–1334), finding life too solitary and seeking a more appropriate setting for the Holy See, established himself at Avignon in 1316. He ordered a "New Palace" to be attached to the "Old Palace" which had been constructed by Benoit XII.

Meanwhile the Cardinals, finding no homes in the papal city of Avignon worthy of their rank, crossed the bridge to Villeneuve-les-Avignon. They built fifteen opulent palaces called "Livrées" and enhanced them with magnificent Florentine gardens. They heaped benefits upon the little village and filled its religious establishments with such gorgeous art objects that they became veritable museums.

In 1322, Cardinal Arnaud de Via, nephew of Pope Jean XXII and one of the wealthiest prelates of the Church, gave orders for the construction of such a "Livrée." In 1333, two years before his death, he presented his palace to a chapter of Canons with orders that they establish a Priory.

The Canons constructed a quadrangular cloister in the courtyard of the palace. They added a dormitory wing and a tower as well as a church in which they entombed the Cardinal de Via's remains. (His crest may be found today on the keystone of one of the side chapels in the church.) Some of the exceptional art works belonging to the Cardinal were placed in the church, including magnificent paintings and a fourteenth-century ivory polychrome Virgin which is considered to be one of Villeneuve-les-Avignon's most beautiful treasures.

In 1789, the Revolution put an end to all this aristocratic and ecclesiastical wealth. The Canons' holdings were confiscated as state property. The cloister, Florentine Garden, and dormitory wing were separated from the church and converted successively into a private school, a gentleman's residence, and a boarding-house for artists. Finally, in 1943, it was purchased by its present hosts, Monsieur and Madame Mille, who restored its original atmosphere, preserved its furnishings, rehabilitated its gardens, and revived the tranquility of ancient days to create in Cardinal de Via's former "Livrée" what is today one of France's outstanding intimate hotels.

CHÂTEAU DE ROUMÉGOUSE

An historical château for the traveler on a modest budget.

If the historical origin of the Château de Roumégouse may seem at times obscure, it is geographically a place of fascination. The castle is placed in the center of a region containing the subterranean river at Padirac, two magnificent canyons, steep hills filled with prehistoric caves and grottoes, and one of the most celebrated scenes of religious pilgrimage in all Christianity—Roc Amadour.

Perhaps the derivation of the name Roumégouse gives a hint of the beginnings of the château. The name stems from the word *roumieu*—pilgrim from Rome—used as a title of glory and fame for those who had been pilgrims in this era when the trip to Rome was made on foot. Very logically a man might have bestowed his honorary name on his home to signal his own religious achievements to other pilgrims passing on the way to Roc Amadour.

In the tenth century the property belonged to the Barony of Gramat, but in 987 it was ceded to the Canons serving the Cathedral at Cahors.

During the Middle Ages the house may have been only a grange of the powerful Abbey of Obasine in Bas-Limousine which possessed many such farm properties in the region of Roc Amadour.

In the fourteenth century Roumégouse became a dependency of the Barony of Castlenau and was used as an advance post of Hughes II of Castlenau, Baron of Gramat, one of the most powerful Lords of Aquitaine.

Other owners of the château are the families of Oriole and Aigrefeuille and finally the Fouilhac family, a branch of the Vallon, to whom Roumégouse belonged at the end of the sixteenth century. We note that the Fouilhac of Mordesson constructed a building called the "Mill of Saut" on the land, detaching it from their property at Roumégouse, and adding it to their property at Mordesson, and it is reasonable to assume that the château was the home of Fouilhac, the famous savant-historian of Quercy at the end of the seventeenth century.

After the epoch of feudality, the Lords of Castlenau were forced to divide their holdings. The Château de Roumégouse passed successively into the hands of divers owners, none of whose names can be found.

Near the beginning of the nineteenth century however, Roumégouse belonged to the Cavalié family who inhabited it for nearly a century, though by 1893 only one part of the castle remained in good estate. M. J. Pisier, husband of Victorine Cavalié renovated it as we see it today. The windows and doors of the Middle Ages were converted into the architectural style of the late Gothic period and the beautiful tower was restored. A park with a plantation of pines was traced, and a terrace encrested with the entwined initials PC (Pisier-Cavalié) was built facing the quiet hills toward Roc-Amadour and the vast calcium plateau of Gramat.

In 1945, the Château de Roumégouse was converted to a hotel, permitting today's traveler to enjoy this lovely restoration and to find respite just as did the ancient "pilgrim from Rome."

CHÂTEAU ST. JEAN

*Site of the historic Isle upon which the great Empire of
Charlemagne was dissolved.*

The Château de St. Jean is a handsome example of "Belle Epoch" architecture. Its broad terrace sweeps down to the Saône. From its front windows one can see the little Isle of St. Jean (known also as the Isle of Palm). Once part of the property of the château, it is the true repository of the important history attached to this place. Some modern writers have advanced the theory that 368,000 Helvetians used the island as a passageway across the River Saône after they had burned their four hundred mountain villages. The age of the territory is gauged by the fact that at Solutré, five miles from the château, archaeological findings reveal the existence of civilizations dating from 15,000 to 12,000 B.C. There is also concrete evidence of Neolithic Period and Bronze Age cultures.

Placed in the heart of Burgundy where the *great* white wines are nurtured, the château and its historic Isle have been the scene of many dramatic events. With the death of Charlemagne in 814, the Empire fell upon troubled times. His son, Louis I, Le Débonnaire, became Emperor of the West. Married first to Irmingarde, by whom he had three sons, he later took as a wife Judith of Bavaria by whom he had a fourth son, Charles II, Le Chauve (832–877). Devoted to learning and pious work, the great St. Louis was constantly caught in the rivalries of his sons, Lothaire I (Emperor of the West, 840), Pépin (King of Italy, 814 to 838), and Louis II (King of Francs, 817 to 843). He finally met his death during an expedition designed to quell the ambitions of Pépin. Lothaire ascended the throne only to be subjugated by the combined forces of his brothers, Charles II and Louis II.

The notoriety of the Isle of St. Jean stems from this moment in history, for it was the scene of a conference held by the three sons of St. Louis, establishing the basis of the Treaty of Verdun by which the Empire of Charlemagne was dismembered into three parts.

In 1210, the Isle was given to the Abbey of Tournus by William II, Count of Macon, and a chapel was built. Pillaged and destroyed by the Protestants in 1562, the Isle is mentioned in the records of the Assembly at Macon, which commanded that "it be razed" for harboring enemies of the state. Today only vestiges of the chapel remain.

Little more is known of the property until 1816 when the Marquis de Barbentane built the present château. The property and vineyard flourished and were enlarged in 1839 by his son. Lovely pavilions were added to its entrance in 1845 and through its gates came all the nobility of the century. Its grounds were the scene of regal receptions until World War II, when all gaiety was set aside. During the war the Marquis de Barbentane, mayor of St. Jean-Le-Priche, was cited by the commune. The plaque, affixed to the gateposts of the château, reads "for courageous, dignified attitudes during the last days of the occupation."

By his strength of character the town and the château were preserved. Today we may repose and reflect on the beauties of the spot where in another day the mighty Empire of Charlemagne met its end.

CHÂTEAU DE LA TORTINIÈRE

A gem in every way.

At the entry of the park, bordering the wall of the property of La Tortinière, are traces of an ancient Roman roadway leading from Tours to Montbazon. It is interesting to speculate whether Saint Martin himself, once a Roman Legionnaire, might not have passed by this hillock overlooking the Indre River. Today, it is the site of a charming, intimate château set in the beautiful landscape of Touraine.

For centuries the area has been given over to the cultivation of the vine and of fruits. But in addition to its excellent agricultural reputation, it has been recognized as a great cultural center.

In the eighth century Tours was the apex of the art of illumination and calligraphy flourishing under the great monk, Alcuin. This eminent scholar, brought from Italy by Charlemagne, became the head of a model educational institute set up at the palace. Later, as Abbot of Tours, Alcuin formed a school for copyists. Masterpieces issued from its doors which today are the pride of the National Library of France.

During the fifteenth and sixteenth centuries the great silk industry, encouraged by the interest of Louis XI, reached its peak. Touraine became the hub of a world of craftsmen and intellectuals. Its capital, Tours, was inhabited by eighty thousand persons who were involved as artists, sculptors, cloth and tapestry weavers, stained glass painters, and goldsmiths. Its countryside became the playground of kings.

The property of La Tortinière is found at Montbazon, a town formed around a keep (tower-like dungeon) built by Foulques Nerra, who also figured in the history of Château d'Artigny. Built at the end of the eleventh century, the keep was installed on the grounds belonging to the Monks of the Abbey of Cormery. Near La Tortinière one can still see the remains of a feudal knoll where the "Black Knight" established himself during the construction of the keep.

The property belonged next to a branch of the Rohan family. During the thirteenth and fourteenth centuries, when a period of happiness and prosperity overtook all Touraine, they ordered a lordly mansion to be built dominating the Valley of the Indre. The broad trees of its park later shaded the promenades of Charles Perrault author of "La Belle Au Bois Dormant" . . . "Sleeping Beauty." Popular opinion affirms that these walks under the broad spreading oaks, now tricentenarians, strongly inspired this author, who also gave us the legendary "Cinderella," "Red Riding Hood," "Puss In Boots," and "Bluebeard."

From this old mansion stemmed, in 1867, the actual Château de la Tortinière built by the Count de Rigny of the celebrated Touraine family Rigny-Usée. (Their château near Chinon, with its Renaissance chapel and its terraces, is still one of the glories of fifteenth-, sixteenth-, and seventeenth-century architecture and landscaping.)

The design of the Château de la Tortinière was inspired by the pretty buildings of the Renaissance mixed with some principals of construction popular at the end of the last century called "Belle Epoch." Once the childhood home of its present hostess, Madame Olivereau, it was converted to a hotel in 1954 by her parents.

Enchanting and white, its round towers gleaming in the sun, it awakens in the beholder all the visions of childhood and one seems to wait, without knowing why, for that breathless moment when "The Sleeping Beauty" will descend the terrace of "La Tortinière."

CHÂTEAU DE TRIGANCE

The dining room, music, and food take one back to medieval days.

From the mountain de Breis, a peak rises up more than 4000 feet, and drops to the east where the mountain range opens up to give us the Grand Canyon of Verdon. Here, in a landscape where viewpoints are astonishing and unforgettable, we find the Château de Trigance, successively the holding of the Monks of St. Victor of Castellane and then of the family Raimondy, who received the land in 1393. Less than a hundred years later it was joined by marriage alliance with the lands of the Demandols, the Castellane, and the Brignole. (The family name of the Princess of Monaco of Château de Betz).

The place must have been inexpugnable. High towers and strong ramparts defended it on three sides, and on the fourth it was defended by the rock itself. There its façade juts out, showing a door carved out of the rock. As in the past, access to this doorway must be made on foot on a roadway of hairpin curves built into the defensive walls. The pathway has been modernized to some extent with a stairway and the ancient ruin is now a remarkable medieval restoration.

To reach the château, one crosses the bridge over the Jabron stream. On the way up the visitor passes a pretty Renaissance pavilion and a thirteenth-century church which possesses a bell tower covered with polychrome tiles. The construction of this church is attributed to the Templars. The entire village of Trigance is a tangle of colorful streets, with a cheerful little square, a high fountain, a thick-set belfry of iron, curious wells in the middle of the street, ramparts, and old doors marked with their ancient dates of placement. On a threshold in the street is the sculptured insignia of a "field marshal" once attached to the great château. The town still retains its feudal aspect since no new houses have been built in modern times. Above the town, 800 feet from the château, is the Chapel of St. Roch with its portico containing three openings, half closed by a lattice of wood. Inside is a large and very old fresco of St. Roch and St. Clair. The earth floor is strewn with pieces of money thrown there by passers-by crossing the Canyon of Verdon. Each week the Prioress comes to gather these offerings destined for the lights of the feast days.

Above the chapel the château itself comes into view. Three towers still stand and strongly mark its angles. The northwest tower was constructed in 1108, and the northeast and south date respectively from the fifteenth and sixteenth centuries.

Today a vast maze of rooms, subterranean passages, corridors, staircases, oubliettes, and cisternes reveal the importance of the place. The towering vaulted rooms, the majestic staircases, the beautiful terrace encircled by mountains, the view far across Castellane—all has been rediscovered and restored. The rehabilitation offers the visitor a chance to feel the serenity of this château that clings to the very earth and rock into which it is built. Its massive solidity imparts to the newcomer the same sense of safety and comfort it must have imparted to the great medieval lords of Provence.

CHÂTEAU DE LA VALLÉE BLEUE

*A very comfortable spot. The hosts convey the feeling
that you are visiting old friends.*

George Sand, with whose name the Château de la Vallée Bleue is unalterably linked, once described its lovely surroundings:

"This lovely blue color which becomes purple and nearly black during the shadowy daytime" . . . the Valley of the Creuse.

The property of the château dates from the fifteenth century, and an oak estimated to be 400 to 500 years old stands at the gates. It was originally mentioned by Julius Caesar in his commentaries as being "the refuge of brigands" (we appreciate the fact that the hearty Berrychons might have *inconvenienced* the invaders). During the Middle Ages the village of St. Chartier was the center of the activities of the Monk Carterius from whom the place takes its name.

A feudal castle was constructed on the site, fortified and circumscribed by a moat. It possessed dependencies as well as the Forest of St. Chartier. Years later, the château and its environs were celebrated by George Sand in her famous romantic novels, "The Master Bell-Ringers," "The Haunted Pool," "Francis the Waif," and "Fanchon the Cricket."

Though born in Paris this famous writer passed forty-four years of her life at the home of her grandmother, the Château of Nohant, in Berry. She heard there the natural language of the peasants which she used so notably in her writing. Never forgetting the songs of the birds and the shouts of the laborers of her childhood, she returned at agitated periods of her life to the calm and equilibrium of the familiar countryside. Married unsuccessfully to Baron Dudevant, from whom she separated after the birth of her two children, she took up "la vie Bohème," encircling herself at Nohant with lovers and friends. Such great artists as Jules Sandeau, Alfred de Musset, Chopin, Liszt, Flaubert, Balzac, Delacroix, Gautier, and Dumas, Fils lived and worked near this fascinating woman. It is this magnetism which was responsible for the building of the Château de la Vallée Bleue.

In 1830, Dr. Pestel, wishing to be near his famous patient, purchased the property called "Le Clé." Judging the old château which stood on the land to be too modest, he ordered it to be destroyed and replaced by an edifice with more allure . . . the actual Château de la Vallée Bleue of today. When the mansion was completed it was the scene of grand and gay reunions which brought together all the intellectual and artistic elite of the period. Dr. Pestel's patient, George Sand, with her coterie of adoring literary and musical followers, was always the star of the event.

The property was left to Dr. Pestel's daughter, whose children later divided the property into four equal parts. In 1961, it was sold by the last remaining grandson of Dr. Pestel to the present hosts of Château de la Vallée Bleue.

Less than 100 years after her death, George Sand's home at Nohant has become a museum and we can view the rooms in which she lived and worked. A few minutes away, at the Château de la Vallée Bleue, we can stay at the same place where the creative luminaries of nineteenth-century France vacationed with George Sand.

A NOTE ON WINES

First-hand advice from Charles Colin, the world's greatest wine taster.

To write of French cooking without a short discourse on wine is unthinkable. Charles Colin, the world's greatest wine taster, eighty-four-year-old Sommelier at Hostellerie de la Poste in Avallon has been tasting wine for seventy years, and he offers the following advice:

"There is no ideal combination. Each menu presents a fresh challenge. As a general rule, one should start a meal with the lightest wines and end with the full-bodied ones. My usual advice is to drink old wines in restaurants and build up one's own cellar with younger vintages. When you buy wine that is very expensive, it is not necessarily a good buy. A good cellar is not built up on price alone."

The proper way to taste wine is to smell it first. Next a sip of wine should be taken and rolled over the tongue. The wine should be "chewed" and allowed to rest in the mouth before being swallowed.

Mr. Colin scorns fancy bottles and fancy glasses. He prefers a big, clear glass that shows the color of wine, deep enough to release the bouquet of the wine when half-filled.

Tourist Facts

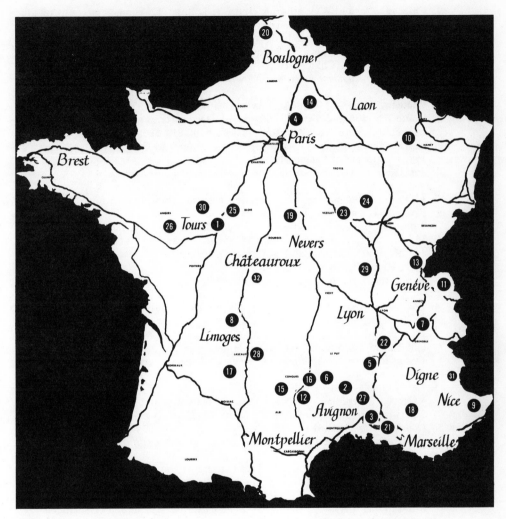

TOURIST FACTS

1. **Château d'Artigny**—Montbazon (Indre-et-Loire). 12 kilometers south of Tours near Route N. 10. Telephone (47) 56-21-77. Open all year. 55 rooms. 2 persons, private bath, $12–$28. 2 persons, private bath, including meals, $16–$23 per person. Menu $5.50–$7.75 à la carte. Service and Tax 20% additional. (Château-Hotel)*
France's most opulent hotel in a beautiful setting. Excellent cuisine.

2. **Château d'Ayres**—Meyrueis (Lozère). 1 kilometer from the crossing of Route RN. 586 and 596. Telephone 10. Open from Palm Sunday to September 30. 22 rooms. 2 persons, private bath, $10–$20. 2 persons, private bath, including meals, $12–$20 per person. Menu $4–$6. Service and Tax 15% additional. (Château-Hotel)*
Just the spot if you are looking for rest and attractive surroundings.

3. **L'Oustau de Baumanière**—Les Baux-en-Provence (Bouche-du-Rhône). Near Route RN. 7 and RN. 113. Telephone 7 or 27. Open all year. 20 rooms. 2 persons, private bath $16–$18. 2 persons, private bath, including meals, $45 per day for 2 persons. Menu $4–$8, Service and Tax included. Rooms and meals are also available at *Cabro d'Or, Relais* of L'Oustau de Baumanière. Rates slightly lower. (Château-Hotel)*
Pure luxury from the dining room to the setting.

4. **Château de Betz**—Betz (Oise). Near Route RN. 2 and 322. Telephone 4-32 or 33. Open all year. 20 rooms. 2 persons, private bath, $12–$15. 2 persons, private bath, including meals, $25 per person. Menu $6–$7. Service and Tax 15% additional. (Château-Hotel)*
One of the most beautiful parks in France. Delightful and 1 hour from Paris.

5. **La Cardinale**—Baix (Ardèche). Route RN. 86. 29 kilometers south of Valence. Telephone 7. Closed January, February, and March. 20 rooms. 2 persons, private bath, $15–$20. Menu $5–$8. Service and Tax included. (*Relais de Campagne*)†
A charming and quiet place combining good food and beautiful rooms.

6. **Château de la Caze**—Gorges du Tarn (Lozère). Route RN. 107. Telephone 1 La Malène exchange. Open from Palm Sunday to October 15. 15 rooms. 2 persons, private bath, $12–$19. 2 persons, private bath, including meals, $15–$20 per person. Menu $5—à la carte, Service and Tax included. (Château-Hotel)*
One of the most historically striking and architecturally beautiful castle-hotels in France.

7. **Château de Challes**—Challes-les-Eaux (Savoie). 6 kilometers south of Chambéry. Open from May 15–September 25. 92 rooms. 2 persons, private bath, $5–$9. Rooms for 2 persons, private bath, including meals, $8–$10 per person. Menu $3–$4. Service and Tax included. (Independent)‡
A comfortable, pleasant hotel with a glorious view of the Alpes.

8. **Château de Cheronnac**—Cheronnac (Haute-Vienne). 4 kilometers from N. 675. Near D. 87 or D. 34. 11 kilometers from Rochechouart. Telephone 2. 15 rooms. 2 persons, private bath, $12–$14. Menu $5—à la carte. Service and Tax included. (*Relais de Campagne*)†
The quintessance of luxury in the heart of France's region of skilled craftsmen.

9. **Château de la Chèvre d'Or**—Eze Village (Alpes-Maritime). Near Route RN. 564. Enter from Nice or Monte-Carlo. Telephone 82-06-16. 7 rooms. 2 persons, private bath, $5–$24. 2 persons, private bath, including meals, $28–$36. Service and Tax 15% additional. (Château-Hotel)*
The view alone is worth a trip from Paris. Delectable food.

10. **Château Choiseul**—Stainville (Meuse). Route N. 4 between Paris and Strasbourg. Telephone 115. Open all year. 13 rooms. 2 persons, private bath, $6–$16. 2 persons, private bath, including one meal and breakfast, $27. Menu $3–$6. Service and Tax included. (*Relais de Campagne*)†
A charming château with a first class table.

11. **Château de Coudrée**—Sciez (Haute-Savoie). Near Route RN. 5. Close to Evian. Telephone 33. Open from May 1 to November 1. 12 rooms. 2 persons, private bath, $6–$16. Menu $5–$7. Service and Tax included. (Château-Hotel)*
Beautifully situated and artistically fascinating. A must if you are traveling with children.

12. **Château de Creissels**—Creissels (Aveyron). Near Millau. Telephone 16. Open June 1 to September 15. 13 rooms. 2 persons, private bath, $3–$6. 2 persons, private bath, including meals, $12 per day for 2 persons. Menu $2. Service and Tax 15% additional. (Independent)‡
An interesting building. Family-type meals. Comfortable. Not for luxury seekers. Warm welcome.

13. **Château de Divonne**—Divonne-les-Bains (Ain). 18 kilometers from Geneva. Telephone 32. Closed from January to Easter. 42 rooms. 2 persons, private bath, $6–$16. 2 persons, private bath, including meals, $26–$36. Tax and Service 25% additional. Menu $5–$7. (*Relais de Campagne*)†
Gracious living in the holiday atmosphere of a French Spa.

14. **Château Fère-en-Tardenois**—Fère-en-Tardenois (Aisne). Near Route N. 367. 46 kilometers from Reims. Telephone 113. Closed from January 3 to February 15. 18 rooms. 2 persons, private bath, $5–$9. 2 persons, private bath, including breakfast and 1 meal, $21–$25 for 2 persons. Menu $4–$6. Service and Tax 15% additional. (*Relais de Campagne*)†
Delectable food. Comfortable rooms.

15. **Château de Lévezou**—Salles-Curan (Aveyron). Near Route N. 111. 35 kilometers northwest of Millau. Telephone 16. Open from March 15 to November 1. 16 rooms. 2 persons, private bath, $3–$4. 2 persons, private bath, including meals, $6 per person. Menu $2–$4. Service and Tax included. (Château-Hotel)*
Although the rooms are small the food is high on my list.

16. **Château de La Malène et Montesquiou**—La Malène (Lozère). Route RN. 107 Gorge du Tarn. Telephone 12. Open from March 15 to November 1. 12 rooms. 2 persons, private bath, $10–$15. Menu $3—à la carte. Service and Tax included. (Château-Hotel)*
The beautiful dining room and food are worth the stop.

17. **Château de Mercuès**—Mercuès (Lot). Off Route N. 111. 8 kilometers north-west of Cahors. Telephone 1 and 30 at Mercuès. Closed from October 15 to Palm Sunday. 24 rooms. 2 persons, private bath, $12–$15. 2 persons, private bath, including meals, $25–$27. Service and Tax included. (*Relais de Campagne*)†
With a dominating view of the Lot Valley, Mercuès is a must.

18. **Château de Meyrargues**—Meyrargues (Bouche-du-Rhône). Near Route N. 7 and N. 96. Telephone 32. Closed the first two weeks in January. 3 rooms. More being added. 2 persons, private bath, $5–$11. 2 persons, private bath, including meals, $12–$24 per person. Menu $6–$7. Service and Tax 18% additional. (Independent)‡
This castle has to be seen to be believed. The food is first rate.

19. **Château de Mimont**—Pouges-les-Eaux (Nièvre). Near Route RN. 7 and RN. 77. Telephone 83-68-21-92. Open all year. 10 rooms. 2 persons, private bath, $16–$30. Menu $6–$7. Service and Tax 20%. (Château-Hotel).*
A rare opportunity to live en famille *among exquisite antiques.*

20. **Château de Montreuil**—Montreuil-sur-Mer (Pas-de-Calais). Route N. 1. 37 kilometers south of Boulogne. Telephone 002. Closed from the middle of September to the middle of December. 20 rooms. 2 persons, private bath, $8–$12. Menu $4–$6. Service and Tax included. (*Relais de Campagne*)†
The flowers and gardens are a sight to behold. A comfortable stopover.

21. **La Petite Auberge de Noves**—Noves (Bouche-du-Rhône). 13 kilometers south of Avignon. Telephone 221 or 451 Châteaurenard. Open all year. 18 rooms. 2 persons, private bath, $7–$12. 2 persons, private bath, including breakfast and one meal, $13–$18 per person. Menu $7—à la carte. Service and Tax 24% additional. (*Relais de Campagne*)†
A must on the southern trip. Magnificent food and first-class accommodations.

22. **Château de Pilate et Fontager**—Ponsas (Drome). On Route RN. 7. 2 kilometers south of St. Vallier. Telephone 119 to St. Vallier. Open all year. 11 rooms. 2 persons, private bath, $6–$9. Menu $4–$8. Service and Tax 15% additional. (Château-Hotel)*
One of the most historically interesting châteaux along the road. Pleasant surroundings.

23. **Hostellerie de la Poste**—Avallon (Yonne). Route RN. 6. Telephone 448. Closed in December and January. 30 rooms. 2 persons, private bath, $11–$16. Menu à la carte. Service and Tax 15% additional. (Château-Hotel)*
To go to France and not dine at Poste, I consider a crime.

24. **Château de Prangey**—Prangey (Haute-Marne). 15 kilometers south of Langres on the road to Dijon. Telephone 1. Closed first two weeks in January. 11 rooms. 2 persons, private bath, $7–$11. Menu $5—à la carte. Service and Tax included. (*Relais de Campagne*)†
A charming château with a pretty park in a restful atmosphere.

25. **Château de Pray**—Amboise (Indre-et-Loire). Telephone 4-66. 16 rooms. 2 persons, private bath, $5–$8. 2 persons, private bath, including meals, $9–$12 per person. Menu $4–$5. Service and Tax included. Open all year. (Independent)‡
A delightful spot providing the traveler with everything he wants.

26. **Hostellerie du Prieuré**—Chênehutte-les-Tuffeaux (Maine-et-Loire). Near Route RN. 751. 8 kilometers from Saumur. Telephone (41) 51-01-01. Closed from January 8 to February 8. 28 rooms. 2 persons, private bath, $9–$12. 2 persons, private bath, including meals, $12–$14 per person. Menu $4.70–$5.70—à la carte. Service and Tax 15% additional. (Château-Hotel)*
The view of the Loire from the dining room is part of the joy.

27. **Le Prieuré**—Villeneuve-les-Avignon (Gard). Near Route RN. 7, 1 kilometer from Avignon. Telephone 81-20-31. Closed from November 1 to February 1. 25 rooms. 2 persons, private bath, $12–$24. Menu from $6 and à la carte. Service and Tax included. (Château-Hotel)*
This charming place provides the traveler with the finest.

28. **Château de Roumégouse**—par Gramat (Lot). Telephone 1 Rignac. 15 rooms. Open all year. 2 persons, private bath, $6. 2 persons, private bath, including meals, $7 per person. Menu $3–$5. Service and Tax 15% additional. (Independent)‡
This place is for the tourist looking for modest accommodations. Family-type meals.

29. **Château St.-Jean**—St. Jean-le-Priche (Saône et Loire). 7 kilometers north of Macon. Telephone 9 to Sennecé-les-Macon. Open all year, 18 rooms. 2 persons, private bath, $6–$13. 2 persons, private bath, including meals, $10–$18 per person. Menu $4—à la carte. Service and Tax included. (Independent)‡
A pleasant stopover in the middle of the white wine district.

30. **Château de la Tortinière**—Montbazon en Touraine (Indre-et-Loire). Near Route N. 10. 8 kilometers from Tours. Telephone Tours 56-20-19. Closed December, January, and February. 20 rooms. 2 persons, private bath, $12–$18. 2 persons, private bath, including meals, $16–$18 per person. Menu $5—à la carte. Service and Tax included. (*Relais de Campagne*)†
A gem in every way. One of the best.

31. **Château de Trigance**—Trigance (Var). Near Route N. 7. South of Castellane on the route from Cannes or Grasse going north. Telephone 18. Closed in November. Mainly a restaurant. Adding a few rooms. Write first. Menu $4—à la carte. Service and Tax 15% additional. (Château-Hotel)*
A rare experience. The dining room, music, and food are only topped by the view.

32. Château de la Vallée Bleue—St. Chartier (Indre).   Near routes RN. 718 and 143.   Telephone 31.   Open all year.   12 rooms.   2 persons, private bath, $5–$6.   Menu $3–$4.   Service and Tax included.   (Château-Hotel)*
A very comfortable spot that gave me the feeling I was visiting dear friends.

* *Château-Hotel Association*, 11 Rue La Boetie, Paris 8, France, or 1361 Madison Ave., N.Y. 10028 Suite 4E.
† *Relais de Campagne*, c/o Hostellerie La Cardinale, Baix (Ardèche) France.
‡ *Independent*, proprietors with no affiliation.   Contact the French Tourist Board in your area.

INDEX